This book is both a cautionary tale and hopeful manifesto. On the one hand, it pointedly warns pastors of misplaced identity and unhealthy expectations. On the other hand, it lays out clear and practical principles for developing the right priorities in ministry. I walked away thinking, where was this book when I started in ministry?

—Brandon D. Smith,
editorial director, Center for Baptist Renewal;
host, Church Grammar podcast;
elder at City Church (Murfreesboro, TN)

Senkbeil and Woodford know what they are talking about. As seasoned pastors and church leaders, they argue that spiritual disciplines (for example, prayer, worship, and reading the Bible devotionally) are the *sine qua non* of pastoral ministry. The Holy Spirit promises to work through the word and Sacraments to form pastors who care for souls—that is, pastors who have a Christ-like character and temperament. Pastoral leadership and strategic planning are important—and the book is chock-full of practical examples. But these ministry tasks remain in their God-given place. They are penultimate, never ultimate. Both the newly ordained and seasoned veterans will profit from the wisdom in this book!

—Reed Lessing,
senior pastor of St. Michael Lutheran Church
(Fort Wayne, IN);
coauthor of *Prepare the Way of the Lord:
An Introduction to the Old Testament*

In *Church Leadership & Strategy* Pastors Woodford and Senkbeil offer an honest and transparent assessment of the realities and pressures of modern pastoral ministry. Weaving together practical suggestions, lessons from experience, and an array of resources, *Church Leadership & Strategy* helps shape servant-leaders for healthy and holistic pastoral ministry.

—Michael W. Newman,
president of the Texas District of the
Lutheran Church—Missouri Synod;
author of *Hope When Your Heart Breaks:
Navigating Grief and Loss*

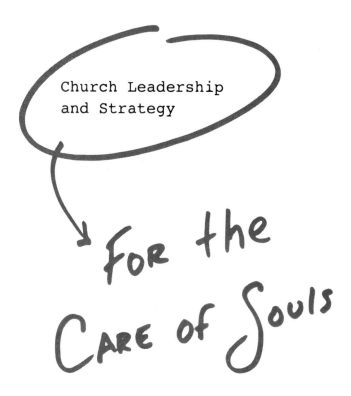

Church Leadership
and Strategy

For the Care of Souls

Lexham Ministry Guides

Foreword by
Brian Croft

Vol. 1

Church Leadership
and Strategy

For the
Care of Souls

Harold L. Senkbeil
and Lucas V. Woodford

LEXHAM PRESS

Church Leadership & Strategy: For the Care of Souls
Lexham Ministry Guides

Print ISBN 9781683593157
Digital ISBN 9781683593164

Lexham Editorial: Todd Hains, Eric Bosell, Erin Mangum
Cover Design: Micah Ellis
Typesetting: Abigail Stocker

Contents

Sidebars

Series Preface

We're impatient.

We want answers now: How do I make lasting friendships? How do I lead my church? How do I raise my kids? Why has this terrible thing happened?

We want success now: that higher-paying job, deeper relationships, bigger churches, healthier churches, more influence.

But our Lord doesn't call us to success, as if the results were up to us. "Neither he who plants nor he who waters is anything, but only God who gives the growth" (1 Cor 3:7). Our Lord asks us to be faithful laborers.

Nor does our Lord expect us to have the answers: "I will give you a mouth and wisdom" (Luke 21:15). Jesus, the eternal Word of the Father, is the Answer who gives us words when we need them and when our neighbors need them. After all, Jesus sees deeper into our hearts than we do; he knows what we need.

The Lord our God creates, redeems, and sanctifies merely by his words. He could give us success and answers now, but he usually doesn't. We learn over time through challenges and frustrations—even Jesus grew over time (Luke 2:52).

Wisdom cannot be bought. It's not a to-do list or clickbait. The authors in this series weren't born with the silver spoon of wisdom in their mouth. They fought for it, clawing it together from the nitty-gritty of experience—by our Lord's word and Spirit.

You won't find plug-and-play answers in this book. You'll need to cogitate and talk with others about it before applying it to your own context.

Wisdom takes time.

Foreword

Pastors are leaving the ministry in droves. Recent statistics reveal that 50 percent of current pastors will not be in the ministry in five years and 80 percent will not be pastors in ten years. But it doesn't stop there. Approximately 4,000 churches close every year, 1,000 alone in my Southern Baptist context. Needless to say, we as evangelicals have a major crisis on our hands. There are many different efforts to explain this reality and try to create solutions. The problem is many of these modern day proposed solutions to salvage these losses are actually aggravating the problem more. Here are two examples.

The first example is the strategy of pragmatism. This is the effort of pastors and church leaders to do whatever is necessary to bring their desired result. Christ and biblical truth no longer become the driving force and foundation of building the church—whatever works to our desired result does. As you can imagine, this often creates a church built on entertainment, consumerism, flashy programs, and shallow spiritual growth working to the ultimate aim of gaining as many new attenders and members as possible.

The second example is the strategy of personality leadership. Leadership is a necessary function in any church, but this strategy takes the need for healthy balanced leadership to an unhelpful level. This strategy focuses on the leader himself, instead of the leader's ministry of the word and care of others. This solution relies more on the winsome, clever tactics of leadership, instead of that leader seeing his role as one to facilitate ministry and soul care in the church. This strategy often creates a CEO top down structure of leadership that relies too heavily on a certain leader and takes the focus off gospel ministry being about the care of others.

There also exists another unfortunate reality as churches approach unhelpful strategies that exasperate this pastoral fallout problem further. That is, these proposed solutions crush the soul of a real pastor. These models and others like it are not just unbiblical, but they take a man's desire to serve God and calling to shepherd souls and try to make him something he is not—a CEO of a business. Combine with that many pastors' lack of knowledge of self-care in the ministry and this burnout rate should not surprise us.

But there is another way.

There is a way to seek to build healthy, vibrant churches that rely on the ministry of the word as pastors are freed to "preach the word in season and out of season" (2 Tim 4:2). There is an approach where church members are well cared for both physically and spiritually as pastors are encouraged to "shepherd the flock among you" (1 Pet 5:2) with the conviction that pastors will "give an account" to Jesus for every soul under their care (Heb 13:17; 1 Pet 5:1–4). There is a solution where a local church is still led well and organized efficiently without the pastor losing sight of his calling to be a servant like Jesus (Mark 10:43–45) and an example of that service to his flock (1 Pet 5:3).

That's the approach which Harold Senkbeil and Lucas Woodford advocate in this book. Through decades of pastoral experience and their own personal ministry struggles, these men passionately advocate for this biblical approach to local church pastoral ministry. They do so with two concerns: the longevity and flourishing of pastors and the thriving and health of local churches. The balance they capture as they deal specifically with leadership and strategy in this model is accurate, essential, and compelling. They understand leadership, but even more they understand to what pastors are truly and biblically called. There is wisdom and practical help for all pastors in many different stages of ministry and leadership in this little book. Allow it to guide you in your pursuit to lead well and fulfill your ministry to shepherd the flock of God on behalf of the Chief Shepherd (1 Pet 5:2–4).

Brian Croft
Senior Pastor, Auburndale Baptist Church

Preface

Pastoring Christ's sheep and lambs seems to be getting more difficult year by year. You know that, if you are a pastor. That's why we wrote this little book. We've got years of ministry under our belts. We're from two different generations, but we share one vision: pastoral ministry is nothing less than tending Jesus' lambs and sheep, for whom he died and rose again.

Christ Jesus is the Good Shepherd who calls his sheep by name and goes out ahead of them, leading them safely through the valley of the shadow of death—beside quiet waters and into the green pastures of the bounty of his love.

This small volume reflects our conviction that everything in ministry—even parish administration, leadership, and planning—revolves around the care of souls.

This handbook in applied ministry complements *The Care of Souls: Cultivating a Pastor's Heart*. Chapter 1 is the personal story of a near-catastrophic experience with wrong-headed leadership principles—an example of the pastoral depletion syndrome and its remedy, explored in chapter 4. Chapter 2 provides a comprehensive survey of practical tools for leadership and church management, while chapter 3 outlines a sound theological framework for implementing those tools.

Jesus forever remains the chief Shepherd and true Bishop of his church: "You were straying like sheep, but have now returned to the Shepherd and Overseer of your souls" (1 Pet 2:25). Sheep just milling around on their own are a disaster in the making. They need protection. They need guidance. They need leadership. They need feeding. In short, they need shepherding.

That's where you come in.

We pray that what we share in these few pages may encourage you toward excellence and faithfulness in ministry, even as it strengthens you in Jesus' name.

Harold L. Senkbeil and Lucas V. Woodford
Ash Wednesday 2019

CHAPTER 1

Learning from Experience: Leadership Woes

(Lucas V. Woodford)

In 2003 I began my ministry at age 27 as an assistant pastor in a very large congregation. We had 3,300 members with a Lutheran parochial grade school (pre-K–8) of nearly 300 students attached. Between congregation and school, we had about fifty employees and a $2.4 million annual budget. With ministry operations on this scale, leadership is essential. I was part of a solid leadership organization, being one of three full-time pastors with numerous other part-time pastors on staff, as well as around forty teachers and numerous other office and support staff. Though I was only there for two and a half years, I watched as the congregation went through a governance model change and implemented various ministry efforts in a large setting.

I saw upfront the importance of leadership. In fact, our congregation was part of a leadership institute that served as a host site to assist pastors in becoming better pastoral leaders through hands-on experience at our church. At a relatively young age in ministry, I led groups of pastors through my area of ministry responsibility (discipleship, Christian education, and small groups) and explored with them the intricacies of pastoral leadership and teamwork in our large congregation.

So, when I received the call to be senior pastor to Zion Lutheran Church only a short time later, I felt I had the skill set, the ambition, and the readiness to jump into that role at a smaller though still good-sized congregation and school (900 members and 150 students). Being confident in my leadership skills and excited for the new ministry and growing area I was moving to, I set out with great anticipation and confidence. However, I quickly found out the Lord has a way of humbling those who think too much of themselves.

My overconfidence and eager anticipation was met with a congregation and school beset by all kinds of internal strife, organizational disorder, ministry conflict, and personnel troubles. Though I was blessed to serve the saints of Zion for over a decade, the first five years were extremely difficult due to a host of issues, one of which was how I had bought into the lie that the church's success was entirely dependent upon my own leadership. As you will see, I certainly affirm the importance of leadership. But making the success of a church (whatever that may be) hinge upon that one sole factor is dubious business.

THE TANTALIZING CHALLENGE

When I arrived, the congregation was convinced they needed to build a new state of the art church facility and school. In fact, they purchased twenty acres of land to do so just one month after my arrival. The congregation itself was situated in what had become a small but fast-growing bedroom community for the Twin Cities (of Minnesota), in the little town of Mayer. Formerly a farming community, new houses were exploding in three new developments. The congregation was growing and had a wonderful intergenerational mix of farmers and country folk combined with commuters and suburbanites of varying metropolitan mentalities.

But as I quickly found out, the congregation was not united about which property to buy, (they had three possibilities) nor were they agreed on how to pay for this new building project (they had cash on hand for the land, but nothing after that), or even if that building project should be the emphasis of the congregation's ministry.

Adding to this unrest was the well-meaning but misguided efforts of some factions in the congregation to champion one or the other of the various ministries within the congregation by rallying troops to their cause, but which created significant divisions. Combined with this were some long-standing personnel staff conflicts, as well as a significant budget shortfall and mounting debt. So, you can imagine the disharmony and angst it created for me as their new young and inexperienced pastor.

I was quickly sucked into the unhealthy spiral of interaction and dysfunction, which ultimately led to compassion fatigue and burnout that I unhealthily tried to bury deep down in my gut and hide lest I be seen as a failure. Pride is a wicked vice the devil will try to use in order to bring down many a pastor. That is why personal prayer and meditation, confession and absolution with a father confessor, and the regular exercising of your faith (apart from sermon prep or Bible study prep) is essential to combat and treat such attacks of the devil.

PAYING THE PRICE?

I did my best to put on the appearance of a brave leader. I kept reading all the latest leadership books and was a master at putting on my poker face and acting like everything was great though I was being torn up inside. In fact, I kept trying to do more, work harder, and be the leader I thought they wanted and needed, only to find I was creating as many fires as I was trying to put out, and alienating my family along the way.

Paranoia and uncertainty about the future of my ministry and the future of the congregation became my nightly obsession. Under the misbelief that if I worked more, tried harder, and was a better leader people would like me more, I began coming into the office at 3:00 a.m. to start my day and staying until late at night after I had attended the last meeting of the day. Even so, landing on a common and uniting leadership emphasis for the congregation was ever elusive. Strife continued. Factions remained. Sadly, after one congregational meeting a former older staff member walked out of the meeting in anger and intentionally shouldered me, nearly knocking me down the stairs to our exit doors. He justified his action by saying I was full of "piss and vinegar." Unfortunately, no one saw the interaction at the moment of physical contact. I viewed tattling on this individual as unhelpful and so buried it among all the other toxic and volatile unrest I thought a leader was simply supposed to willingly bear and smile about.

I was trying to do absolutely everything by my own reason and strength. I knew the Great Commission, I embraced it, and I was trying to fulfill it, even if it killed me! But the growth wasn't magically happening like all the church growth books said it was supposed to. (Though some of my new member classes were at high levels— thirty-five or more people —many others were quite slim.) Those same books said a leader looking to bring change and vibrancy to his ministry should expect all kinds of resistance and animosity and needs to be prepared to endure some misery in ministry and life. They said this was just the price you should expect to pay if you wanted to lead a change toward a passionate, vibrant, mission-oriented church.

I bought into the misbelief that all the misery I was experiencing was simply what ministry was supposed to be like and was the price of being a leader. Those were some very dark times. In fact, the only friend I thought I had was the hot shower I took in the morning. The devil and our own sinful flesh love to isolate us and attack us with all kinds of false belief, despair, and other great shame and vice.

But this is why what I offer here is my warning to recognize the important but limited role of leadership in ministry. Yes, pastors certainly need to be a leader and know how to think strategically, organizationally, and to balance staff personalities and directives, as well as oversee and ensure things are getting done, or if that is not your strength, find someone who can do those things for the congregation. But to make leadership the hallmark of ministry is to subject Christ

Growth and Conflict

Church revitalization and growth often come at great cost to the pastor. For example:

In his book Direct Hit: Aiming Real Leaders at the Mission Field, Paul D. Borden says: "When leading a congregation of unwilling people to higher levels of effectiveness, risking security and significance demands a courage that may come only through engaging in considerable losses."[1]

See also Thom Rainer's Breakout Churches: Discover How to Make the Leap: "The combination of pastoral tenure and persistence seems to be a powerful combination that God has used to move these churches to greatness. While many of our comparison church leaders had a pattern of leaving churches at the early signs of difficulties and obstacles, the Acts 6/7 leaders recognize that the greatest days for the church may lie just beyond the latest struggle."[2]

One last example is Jock E. Ficken's Change: Learning to Lead and Living to Tell About It. "As congregational leaders, we should not be surprised by the external opposition by forces in our communities. We should not wring our hands in despair nor should we seek always to avoid those forms of opposition."[3]

and his word to your leadership, which is not the nature of the church. Therefore, a word of caution is warranted.

ASPIRING TO LEADERSHIP AT ALL COSTS: A WORD OF CAUTION

During my early years at Zion the congregation retained the services of a professional leadership guru and organizational manager in order to try and help steer the congregation in the right direction. The individual also happened to be affiliated with the same pastoral leadership organization that I assisted at my first and much larger congregation. I worked with this person closely during this time, while also becoming engaged in a year-long contract with another ministry coach to assist myself and the congregation's newly-hired-fresh-from-seminary associate pastor. I was bound and determined I was going to turn things around.

The leadership guru worked with our congregation for about a year, developing a strategic plan and work plan, which was unfortunately crafted in concepts foreign to the congregational leaders and therefore would end up ineffective. In time, after experiencing all the dysfunction and disorder happening internally firsthand, this leadership consultant decided to withdraw from the project, indicating the situation and unrest was just too intense, and that leading the congregation through this was more difficult than first anticipated.

At that point I remember thinking to myself, "Seriously, you've got to be kidding me! I thought leaders were never supposed to back down. And you're the leadership expert? If you're the professional and you want out, where does that leave me? Sure, you get to go and hide from this mess, but I'm still here and still called to serve and love these people." Very quickly I began to think, "Maybe leadership at all costs was not what it was cracked up to be, nor as effective some claimed it to be."

Three years into this ministry setting I was exhausted, terrified, and burned out. Yet, I never let a soul know just how lonely and hurt I was, nor the anguish that was eating me up on the inside. In fact, my anxiety was so high my regular digestive functions stopped working properly for a time. Thus, when the leadership guru bowed out from assisting the congregation, something in me finally snapped. If this leadership guru could not handle the intensity of this congregation's situation and had to drop out, even though all the latest strategic planning techniques and leadership building exercises had been utilized and employed, where exactly did that leave me?

A NEW WAY FORWARD

It was here that I began to see the empty promises of those who made pastoral leadership the end all to be all for ministry. I did not disavow pastoral leadership. Rather I saw it in a new and more proper light. For it was also at this point that I began to see the care of souls and the historic role of the pastor as *physician of the soul* was far more than my ability to be a good leader.

Part of that recognition occurred in the doctoral studies that I was also engaged in at the same time as all this unrest. (Nothing like adding more work to an already chaotic mess). It was here that I was introduced to Professor Harold Senkbeil (who would later become a very dear friend, confidant, and even baptismal sponsor to one of my children). This loving professor and pastor gave me permission to see ministry in a fuller and more historic light, which included profound insight into the care of souls and not just the leading of members. Thus, I began to care more intentionally and classically for the individual souls of the congregation, giving them Jesus as I was called to do, rather than giving them myself, my ingenuity, or my next great idea. I learned that leadership and the care of souls go hand in glove when soul care leads the way.

Resourcing History

The result of Lucas's doctoral studies in Christian outreach can be read in his book <u>Great Commission, Great Confusion, or Great Confession? The Mission of the Holy Christian Church</u> (Eugene, OR: Wipf & Stock, 2012). Lucas explores the latest trends in the North American church in light of a careful analysis and assessment of the Great Commission and the historic confession of the holy Christian church. The New Testament church and historic church valued the word of God and the daily vocations of ordinary people more than a method or technique for growing the church. The contemporary church can follow this dynamic yet simple paradigm for outreach and identity today.

Coupled with the beginnings of a new strategic plan put in theological and leadership language that the congregational leadership could understand, I noticed a shift in my ability to lead and their receptiveness to receive my leadership. It was at this point that I began to recognize the tempered place of leadership, and the need to keep it located in the helpful but limited role it has to play in pastoral ministry. As such, I began to study the larger role of leadership woes in the church and compare it to the historic confession of the church to see how I might use that historic confession to help lead and direct a congregation in the development of a new and more fully developed strategic plan.

A BALANCED APPROACH
TO LEADERSHIP

From this very trying experience I want to offer a word of caution about how pastors might approach and carry out their leadership development in their congregations. Again, please understand I affirm the importance of leadership, but I want you to see it has a specific place and limitation within the pastoral ministry. Pastoral ministry is far larger than the leadership of a pastor.

Even so, for many years the trend and emphasis in the North American church has been on leadership, especially the leadership ability of the pastor. Workshops, courses, and whole institutes have been established around the importance of the leadership of a pastor, which also often promised increased vitality or numerical growth to the local church if pastors would just be the right kind of leader and develop the right kind of strategic plan. As I've already told you, I fully bought into that kind of thinking, though always trying to maintain my theological scruples. Yet I found the promises of this leadership model to be wanting in my own experience. And it took its toll on me emotionally, spiritually, and particularly in terms of my God-given vocations as husband and father.

If leadership is all the church needs in a pastor in order to grow and thrive, what need do we have of the Holy Spirit and the word of God? Even more, as I found out, a congregation can have the best leadership consultants around and still not be able to solve a church's dysfunctions. Being a leader is not what forgives sins, nor does it soothe troubled souls. That is nothing against organizational leadership, it's just demonstrating the limitations of that quality in pastors. The forgiveness of sins comes by the power of God's word and sacraments enacted through the art of caring for the soul as an under-shepherd of Christ. A good pastor will recognize the importance of leadership, but also its limitations. Sometimes leadership must step aside and let Jesus and his word of law and gospel take priority and be enacted.

OTHER CAUTIONARY VOICES

Others in the church have begun making similar realizations. Some have recently recognized the overemphasis on leadership in what might be called "leadership emphasis fatigue." Lance Ford is one such author who addresses this leadership obsession head-on in his thoughtful book, *Unleader: Reimagining Leadership … and Why We Must.*

He laments what he calls a leadership obsession: "Perhaps the biggest mix-up concerning the current leadership obsession is that Jesus himself directly contradicts much—if not most—of what is being imported into the church under the leadership mantra."[4] He makes the case that this leadership obsession often reduces or ignores the servant nature of pastoral ministry and the life of a Christian and calls for true leaders to sit at the feet of a master to gain experience, especially from *the* master Jesus Christ. It is a helpful echo of Pastor Senkbeil's emphasis on the cultivation of a pastoral *habitus*—that is, the pastoral character and temperament, worked by the Holy Spirit through the word and sacraments.

Australian Michael Frost echoes this concern and call for renewed servanthood in a postscript to Ford's book: "I fear we are living through a time in the church's history when once again leadership has been reduced to simple steps or memorable formulas, when authors are purveying models they claim anyone can quickly adopt, and when conference speakers are dishing up five of their seven steps for effective leadership and then encouraging audiences to buy their latest book for the last two steps." Instead, he says, leaders "need to sit for hours on end at their Master's workbench to humble themselves enough to learn, to suffer, to sacrifice, to be shaped into the likeness of the Master Craftsman." [5]

I hope my story convinces you that in order to be an effective leader you need to develop a pastoral *habitus* that includes cultivating the skills of leadership. What I offer below, in chapter 2, will simply be a means to begin thinking strategically and practically about one aspect of that *habitus* and then provide a number of additional book options that you could explore to continue cultivating the aspect of leadership for your pastoral *habitus*.

The Good, the Necessary, and the Ugly Sides of Leadership—How It Nearly Ended My Ministry

(Lucas V. Woodford)

Leadership is one of the hottest topics today. A search for "leadership" on Amazon books reveals over 50,000 results! With that many options what I offer here will invariably be nothing new. Yet I want to provide you with a perspective on pastoral leadership that I had to learn the hard way. This chapter is not just a survey of pastoral leadership resources; in a real way it represents my personal journey of discoveries about leadership as a pastor and the insights gained from my failures and false beliefs about pastoral leadership.

Step one in pastoral leadership is that the church is the Lord's and not mine, that by his precious blood and his holy innocent suffering and death, he redeemed the beloved souls of this world and desires that all be saved and come to the knowledge of truth (1 Tim 2:4). Thanks be to God that fact will never change no matter how great or terrible a leader I may be. My blunders as a pastoral leader or my successes (however they may be defined) can never take away the triumph and victory our Lord achieved by his death and resurrection.

Yet that does not give us permission to be lazy, poor stewards, ignorant, or incompetent in caring for and leading the local congregations we are privileged to serve. Whether a pastor wants to lead or not, by default of his position he is a leader. Should he prefer the titles of shepherd, under-shepherd, pastor, minister, physician of the soul, or preacher, that still does not remove the reality that a pastor is a leader. Whether he leads the liturgy, the Bible class, the elders' meeting, the voters' meeting or the prayer of the church, a pastor is always a leader. The question is not whether you want to be a leader; it's what kind of leader do you want to be?

TWO EXTREMES

Yet, at the same time I have far too often seen pastoral leadership portrayed as the end all and be all of pastoral ministry. Treating leadership as the ultimate factor and essential ingredient in ministry would be a shortsighted and unhelpful mistake. As I already told you, I personally learned that the hard way. A word of caution is needed to help us keep our bearings on Christ and his church rather than on the latest leadership fad.

However, I have also witnessed pastors who despise the idea of pastors taking on the nomenclature or role of leadership associated with the tasks of pastoral work. This, too, is unhelpful. I will readily admit that Jesus does not use the language of leadership as our modern age does. But that does not negate the fact that a pastor has to lead. In fact, many of the things a pastor does fall under the practice of leadership, especially with the logistics and realities of contemporary parish structures. Even the first apostles of the early church had to figure out a way to lead when something as mundane as the logistics of the "daily distribution" was causing problems (Acts 6). Paying attention to leadership enabled the apostles to better focus on ministry. Likewise pastors today need to cultivate good leadership skills, while employing the God-created use of reason to think strategically in order to develop a sound strategic plan of ministry operation for your local church.

In the end, a pastor's primary directive given by the Lord is the correct preaching and teaching of God's word and the faithful administration of the sacraments (Matt 28:18–19). But what that looks like and sounds like at the level of the local congregation in the twenty-first century will certainly have elements of leadership to it, just like it did in the first century.

THE PASTOR WHO LEADS
HIS CONGREGATION

What is central to the pastoral ministry? In *The Care of Souls*, Harold Senkbeil wonderfully identifies the central feature of pastoral ministry as the enactment of the word of Christ upon the souls for whom our Lord shed his blood and died. In today's church climate a pastor is expected to be a jack-of-all-trades while at the same time endeavoring to master the art of the care of souls. Modern job descriptions for pastors often have a laundry list of things he is responsible to do, which extend far beyond the central aspect of administering word and sacrament. This is where it becomes helpful for a pastor to understand what an organizational leader is and how to lead a congregation given his specific ministry setting and the expectations (spoken and unspoken) of his congregation.

Depending on the specific setting, location, size, structure, and staffing of a congregation, a pastor can have any number of additional roles placed upon him by the congregation. Committee meetings, preparing agendas, organizing volunteers, equipping lay leaders, understanding church governance systems and church budgets, working with fellow clergy and nonclergy staff, setting goals for the year, administering congregational operations, handling stress, encouraging the staff around you, and the list goes on and on. Those may not be central to the pastoral care of souls, but you can be sure that if you neglect to do what the congregation expects you to do (at least in some reasonable and competent manner) they will inevitably hinder your care of souls.

Thus, it will be essential and helpful for you to know and understand your congregation's governance structure and constitution. Some constitutions may be more ideal than others, but you nonetheless have to work within the current parameters and policies of your church. You can certainly propose changes later if something is deficient or unhelpful, but for the time being, you have to act in good faith to the congregation and the constitution that established its organizational governance. If you do think changes are warranted, be sure to use the appropriate channels and protocols of the congregation and denominational polity to bring about change. Many structures are board-based, others are policy-based structures. Often, how well such structures work really depends on the elected or appointed lay people in positions of power, and how well they work with the staff and pastors of a congregation, as well as how well a pastor understands, utilizes, and works within the organizational structure of his congregation.

PREPARING TO LEAD:
UNDERSTANDING SELF-INSIGHT

Depending on your specific setting, congregation, and governance structure, you may be asked to do more or less than another pastor in a different setting. For some pastors that's not a big deal and they embrace such a task naturally. Some pastors simply have natural leadership instincts. Others may have experience in leadership roles from other settings of life. But the lack of either of those aptitudes or experiences does not eliminate someone from being a leader. Leadership ability can be aided by the personality and emotional intelligence of a pastor. But it can also be thwarted by those things just the same. Introverts can serve as leaders just as well as extroverts. Yet plenty of

Emotional Intelligence

There are plenty of resources for you to grow good emotional self-awareness and insight. Two are:

- <u>Emotional Intelligence: Why It Can Matter More Than IQ</u> by Daniel Goleman (New York: Bantam, 1995)
- <u>Emotional Intelligence 2.0</u> by Travis Bradberry and Jean Greaves (San Diego: TalentSmart, 2009)

self-styled leaders lacking in self-awareness and insight can destroy a church (or any organization) in no time at all.

One's natural disposition does not automatically remove leadership potential from someone, nor does it automatically make them a competent leader. Rather, whatever one's personality and disposition, it requires an individual to have good emotional intelligence for self-insight. And once some emotional self-awareness is obtained, you can intentionally work at those elements of your personality that may not naturally meld with what may be required of you as a leader. In fact, there are plenty of resources for you to develop self-insight should you wish to explore that option. I list a few in the footnote below.

EXPECTATIONS

When you understand your own emotional intelligence you can see the expectations your congregation has of you in a clearer light. It allows you to better comprehend those expectations given your inclinations and disposition of character. It also allows you to more fully explore the congregation's expectations of you, and for you to communicate your expectations of the congregation's leaders in light of their expectations. When both those expectations are clearly communicated, any needed alternatives can be worked out agreeably for all involved. It also lets you better understand how to manage your time and attend to your daily work with realistic expectations, as well as make requests to the congregation for discussion should they have some unrealistic expectations of you. Bottom line: ignore expectations at your own peril.

Part of my problem was the misbeliefs that I created about my own leadership for the congregation, as well as those expectations I had of myself and my time allotment. They did not arise out of reality, but from an unrealistic ideal and a few hypercritical individuals in the congregation. A few negative individuals can really weigh you

Boundaries

Here are some books to help you set boundaries on your work time and daily task management.

- <u>The 7 Habits of Highly Effective People</u> by Stephen Covey (Simon and Schuster, 1989)
- <u>First Things First</u> by Stephen Covey (New York: Simon and Schuster, 1994)
- <u>Boundaries for Leaders</u> by Henry Cloud (San Francisco: Harper Business, 2013)

Note that while these book are helpful on a practical level, they may not affirm your theology.

One book that draws together biblical thinking and productivity is <u>Every Day Matters: A Biblical Approach to Productivity</u> by Brandon D. Crowe (Bellingham, WA: Lexham Press, 2020).

down, can't they? I found several helpful resources to assist me: 1) see reality more clearly; 2) set realistic boundaries for myself; 3) navigate through what was urgent and not urgent; and 4) sort out what was important from what was not important for my daily schedule (see the books in the "Boundaries" sidebar). Though these books are not theological in nature, they nonetheless help one gain perspective on being a realistic and competent day by day leader.

KNOW YOUR MINISTRY AND
THE TEAM AROUND YOU

As a pastor, you are a servant. But in some settings congregation job descriptions and positions have you as the leader, director, chief, or for lack of a better phrase, the boss who is charged with oversight of multiple other congregation workers. In my first congregation my senior pastor had ultimate oversight (though delegated out) of nearly 50 church workers and employees of the congregation and parochial school. In my most recent congregation, I had ultimate oversight (though delegated out in various forms) of nearly 20 church workers and employees of the congregation and school. One of the major duties of my senior pastor job description states: "The Senior Pastor is to serve the congregation and day school by providing spiritual leadership, pastoral care, administrative oversight and organizational direction to all congregational endeavors, with a broad schedule of worship, music, preaching, teaching and fellowship." This is more specifically enumerated in no less than twelve following duties, the first seven of which are pertinent to this present discussion. My job description read,

The Senior Pastor:

1. Provides vision for the congregation and all its entities as it seeks to provide dynamic ministry for the members of the congregation, the community and the world;

2. Supervises all staff members (not micromanages), called and contracted, in their work and ministry so that there is unity and consensus centered on the vision for the congregation;

3. Works with the congregation officers and boards to build unity around a common vision for the congregation;

4. Works with the budget committee and church council to make sure ministry priorities are funded;

5. Authorizes ministry expenditures that do not exceed the budget;

6. With the appropriate board, supervises, hires and terminates church support staff (this does not include called workers);

7. Promotes new ministry initiatives and gives direction to all congregation boards and committees.

You can see there is much my congregation expected of its senior pastor that goes beyond the central task of soul care through word and sacrament ministry. In my case, there was ample work that needed to be done for the congregation as an organization, but also with and among the other paid workers of the congregation and school. How one accomplishes these tasks does require some leadership ability, specifically the ability to work with teammates in ministry.

THE JOYS AND CHALLENGES
OF TEAM MINISTRY

Putting things bluntly, team ministry can be a blessing and a curse. There is nothing better than working with fellow pastors or coworkers who understand ministry and see ministry the same way as you. But there is also nothing worse than having a fellow pastor or partner in ministry whose personality, priorities, and peculiarities completely rub you the wrong way. Even worse is when your team ministry is filled with competition, jealousy, or animosity among fellow workers. They may agree it's important to love the Lord with all their heart, soul, and mind, and love their neighbor as themselves, but they just can't bring themselves to see each other as a neighbor, let alone see each other as a capable or competent partner in ministry.

I've seen it all. Though I've had a good overall team ministry experience myself, there have been plenty of bumps and challenges along the way. But it's nothing like some of the horror stories I've heard among fellow pastors who could not get along with one another, or pastors who did not know their own place or have a servant's heart, or pastors and teachers who refused to work together for the good of the ministry even though they served the same congregation and school.

In short, team ministry means there is more than one sinner coming together to work collaboratively in the ministry of a congregation. As such, wherever there are two or more sinners gathered there will be people sinned against, personalities clashing, priorities competing, and styles rubbing someone the wrong way. Yes, that might be an opportunity to practice mutual confession and forgiveness, but not all coworkers are ready to be told or even believe they have sinned against you, or that their work ethic, behavior, preaching or teaching style simply drive you crazy.

Hence, it becomes important to understand the basic dynamics of team ministry, personalities, how to regularly communicate, and what it takes to make it through the difficult and yet very rewarding reality of team ministry. It's also important to realize that it's O.K. if people of the congregation or school like a coworker or fellow pastor more than you, just as there will be people in the congregation who like you better than your coworkers for one reason or another. If you become intimidated by that or jealous of it you can bet your team ministry will soon begin to falter.

TEAM BUILDING

Team builder exercises and team collaboration retreats, along with regular meetings are integral to team ministry. Learning to communicate and function as a team is vital to your success and daily interaction. My own experience had plenty of ups and downs but was surrounded with people willing to collectively engage in team ministry in a way that constantly challenged each of us to grow and get better at what we did. Over the years I regularly held twice a year team leadership retreats at the beginning and end of the school year, as well as regular weekly or biweekly meetings during the year with my various leadership and pastoral staff. As part of those retreats and meetings we studied numerous books on the nature of teamwork and leadership among our ministry setting, as well as engaged in varying team building and communication activities. There are numerous online resources and simple team-building activities you can find to develop your team cohesion (for example: folding over a mat while your team is standing on it; building a Lego structure while tied to your teammates with each only having one hand usable; a tallest structure building competition between teams with toothpicks and marshmallows).

Some books are better than others. Many are not necessarily ministry centered but come from a secular business or nonprofit model of teamwork. The key was they afforded good discussion among our team. In the "Team Building" sidebar, I've listed some of the most helpful books my team has used over the last decade.

Additionally, from the start of any team ministry setting it's good to give one another permission to admit that in some ways you will inevitably drive each other crazy and you need to be OK with that, assuming those things that drive you or your fellow workers crazy is nothing sinful or detrimental to ministry. Personalities and styles of interaction and teaching, preaching, and care of souls is going to

Team Building

There are many good books on team building. This list is by no means exhaustive or authoritative.

First, some books by John C. Maxwell. His underlying theology (though not the emphasis in his books) may or may not be compatible with your theological tradition. Take the good and dismiss the unhelpful; the value is in your team's discussion of these books and their principles.

- <u>The 21 Irrefutable Laws of Leadership</u> (Nashville: Thomas Nelson, 1998, 2007)
- <u>The 17 Indisputable Laws of Teamwork</u> (Nashville: Thomas Nelson, 2001)
- <u>Everyone Communicates, Few Connect</u> (Thomas Nelson, 2010)
- <u>The 5 Levels of Leadership</u> (New York: CenterStreet, 2011)

The others include a number by Patrick Lencioni. He writes in an engaging narrative style to present team-building principles.

- <u>The Five Dysfunctions of a Team</u> (San Francisco: Jossey-Bass, 2002)
- <u>Death By Meeting</u> (San Francisco: Jossey-Bass, 2004)
- <u>Politics, Silos, and Turf Wars</u> (San Francisco: Jossey-Bass, 2006)

An essential book for larger team ministry settings is <u>Good to Great</u> by Jim Collins (San Francisco: Harper Collins, 2001). It is geared toward for-profit companies and has a great chapter on leadership. He explores his principles of leadership and organizational goals among nonprofits in <u>Good to Great and the Social Sectors</u> (San Francisco: Harper Collins, 2005).

One last resource for ministry teams to consider is Tom Rath's <u>Strengths Finder 2.0</u> (New York: Gallup Press, 2007). The accompanying online inventory can be used for group discussion about each individual's strengths and how they can be best used in your team's ministry setting.

vary from person to person. The key thing about this is recognizing how you will work through those things for the good of the team, the congregation and the growth of God's kingdom as you care for the souls of your community and congregation.

JOB DESCRIPTIONS AND ACCOUNTABILITY

It will be very helpful for each staff member of your ministry to know what their specific job duties and responsibilities are, as well as what expectations the senior administrative teammate has of each worker. Spell them out in writing if possible and be sure to talk about them collaboratively. Unspoken expectations will always end up being unmet and be a disappointment to someone. You may have a higher standard or much different expectation than your coworker.

Likewise, where appropriate, review the respective position descriptions of coworkers together so that clear expectations and chains of accountability are communicated. Thus, be sure to consider if there are formal job descriptions that accompany each position within the congregation. If not, ask the appropriate boards or committees and staff members to work together to create them or acquire templates or examples of them from your judicatory office. Also explore if there is an understood and clearly established (printed) chain of command or reporting relationship among congregational employees, along with proper procedures or protocols for daily responsibilities, expectations, and organizational flow of responsibilities and powers to be carried out among the congregation's staff members.

COMMUNICATION MODES

Be sure to have open communication right from the start. I cannot stress this enough. Communication is utterly essential for any ministry, especially one based upon communicating the good news of the shed blood of Jesus Christ. Thus, create a weekly information flow and be sure to lead by example. Assess what things went well and what could be done better. Take moments to celebrate various milestones and successes, as well as to explore how to ensure accountability with one another. Extend thank yous and compliments often and liberally. Avoid passive-aggressive forms of communication. In person, up front, tactful, and compassionate communication is always best. Emails or texts have their place and can be used where appropriate, but they also have their pitfalls. Using them for communication of facts is one thing but using them for communicating matters of the heart among your team is another. Such things are best done face to face as tone of voice or actual intent of meaning is often difficult to read unless you are a gifted writer or have a long-standing relationship with the person.

If constructive criticism must be done with an individual for the benefit of the team and/or overall ministry, (whether paid staff or volunteer) take a positive constructive approach that begins with something you appreciate about them, then switches to the constructive criticism, but ends with another positive about the individual. It's what I call the leadership fashion model approach: "Love the hat, not the belt, but I adore those shoes!" When you begin by thanking a teammate for their work or with what you appreciate about them, it helps to disarm them and makes them much more receptive to what issue might need to be addressed and discussed together constructively.

Likewise, if you are responsible for doing job reviews, beware of generic review forms that only offer you choices something like "satisfactory, unsatisfactory, or needs attention". If all you record on an evaluation is the negative elements, without any expression of the positive, you can be sure your work relationship will be severely strained, especially if the coworker or teammate is a sensitive soul. Therefore, be intentional about expressing things you appreciate about your teammates and coworkers on review or evaluation forms or look to amend such forms that allows for intentional affirmation of the worker.

TALKING AND LAUGHING ARE GOOD

Be sure to grow together, read the word together, and where possible, laugh together. Yes, a team that prays together can stay together, but I've also learned from experience that a team that jokes, jests, and laughs together likes to be together and is likely to stay together much longer. Thus, afford time for the sharing of spontaneous or planned (appropriate) humorous stories of life experiences or of recent humorous ministry occurrences. Be sure to model healthy give-and-take or appropriate playful back-and-forth among your team. Also be ready to be an advocate for your team and staff to any leadership board.

In my case, I partnered with the same full-time associate pastor for over eleven years. In fact, he's turned down three opportunities/calls to be pastor elsewhere. We had different strengths and weaknesses, and we had very different interests. Yet we were both committed to our Lord and loved the people of our congregation and community. It was Christ's church and not either one of ours after all. Therefore, we strove to lift each other up and speak well of each other to the congregation, especially if a member would seek to try to divide us or try to gain our favor at the expense of the other. We celebrated ministry milestones with each other, communicated regularly, and were not bothered if a member was more comfortable with one of us or preferred one of us rather than the other. Of course, all of this took time to cultivate and develop, and there were plenty of bumps along the way, and plenty of times we drove each other nuts. But as uncomfortable as it may have been, we always committed to hash things out for the sake of our ministry and the care of our congregation. As a result of such deliberate and consecrated strategies we enjoyed the fruits of the effort and rejoiced in a healthy and long ministry partnership.

Likewise, I was with many of my school teaching staff for the thirteen years I served at Zion. Along with all our ministry staff, I challenged them along the way. I set a vision of ministry in front

Theological Fodder

We also need books of theology and professional growth to spur us on in working together. Lucas has gone through a wide range of materials with his staff, including:

- The Large Catechism by Martin Luther
- Drive: The Surprising Truth About What Motivates Us by Daniel Pink (New York: Riverhead Books, 2009)
- The Benedict Option by Rod Dreher (New York: Sentinel, 2017)

of them, developed a team covenant with them, and asked them to pledge to a culture of excellence and to creating a positive enthusiastic atmosphere that made others want to be around us. We certainly prayed together and studied the word of God together, but we also loved to laugh and joke together. And yes, we were all very different and we could certainly drive each other crazy at times, too. Though there are challenges of team ministry, the joy of shared burdens and collaboration of mutual ministry provides countless opportunities to grow and rejoice with one another.

LEGAL DOCUMENTS AND
REPRESENTATION

Given our litigious society, every congregation should consider retaining an attorney for any number of reasons. If your congregation has any staff handbook or legal employment policies in place, be sure everyone understands them well. Be sure to consult with your congregation's lawyer regarding keeping any needed documents current and up to date with legal employment laws as well as any needed exemption language regarding employment practices and SOGI (Sexual Orientation Gender Identity) laws, or wedding policies of the congregation that you may need your leadership to address formally.

It's sad that churches need to do this, but I was involved in more than a few situations requiring our attorney's services. From hostile community members, to inappropriate behavior of support staff, to false accusations, to simple property and liability issues, our attorney was often needed and helpful. Be sure to do your due diligence for the protection of yourself, your workers, and your congregation.

STRATEGIC PLANNING

Once you understand how congregation governance operates, what specific job duties each employee and called church worker are responsible to carry out, and you have an agreed upon reporting relationship or accountability system (where does the buck stop and why), then you're ready to start considering various organizational short term and long term strategic plans. However, I again want to speak cautiously here; far too many denominations and pastors end up substituting a strategic plan for the theology and mission of the church. Remember what the ultimate purpose and mission of the church is, as well as what remains the heart and center of the church in every local congregation, namely, word and sacrament ministry founded upon the shed blood of Jesus Christ for the salvation of souls.

Nonetheless, since each local congregation has a unique setting, size, location, and structure to its organization, pastors should be mindful of how they can best lead, equip, and utilize the resources of the congregation for the sake of the ministry and the growth of God's kingdom. Remember that growth is far more than mere numbers, that is, a *quantifiable* growth in the roster of your church or how many you have in attendance on an average Sunday. It is also a *qualitative* growth, that is, growth in wisdom and knowledge of the faith and the vocations in which Christians serve. Therefore, it's the pastor's job to be sure he is well acquainted with sound biblical theology, and particularly the theology of his own denomination as he considers various approaches to strategic planning.

Again, there are numerous books to consider when doing strategic planning for the various ministry endeavors a congregation undertakes. Some of the ones I have used to assist my own thinking for strategic planning are listed in the "Strategic Planning" sidebar. Depending on the congregation and ministry setting, a pastor needs to think strategically (at one level or another) about how ministry will be carried out among the saints at his congregation and in the community the congregation is situated. For example, this means a pastor and congregation should think about the location of the church. Is it rural, small town, suburban, city, or inner city, and how does that location impact the ministry of the church? What is the industry or

Strategic Planning

Among the many books on strategic planning, Lucas has used the following for his own ministry setting:

- <u>Multipliers: How the Best Leaders Make Everyone Smarter</u> by Liz Wiseman with Greg McKeon (San Francisco: Harper Business, 2010)
- <u>True North: Becoming an Authentic Leader</u> by Bill George (San Francisco: Jossey-Bass, 2015)
- <u>Start With Why: How Great Leaders Inspire Everyone to Take Action</u> by Simon Sinek (New York: Penguin, 2009)
- <u>Leaders Eat Last: Why Some Teams Pull Together and Others Don't</u> by Simon Sinek (New York: Penguin, 2017)
- <u>Making Vision Stick</u> by Andy Stanley (Grand Rapids: Zondervan, 2007). While Andy Stanley has caused theological controversy, nevertheless, this isn't a theology book. But it was helpful as a reference point for implementing and communicating a formal strategic plan within a congregation.

job makeup of the congregation and community? Likewise, what is the age of the congregation and the average age in the congregation, and how does that impact the ministry of the church? What is the educational makeup of the congregation? How big is the congregation? How active is the congregation? Is it in debt? What shape are the buildings in? Does it have a preschool, a day school, or an association high school? A number of other issues also may impact various aspects of the ministry.

CONGREGATION MENTALITY: F-16S AND CESSNA 172S

Remember every congregation is different. You cannot assume they will act, behave or think the same way. I learned this the hard way as well. The first congregation I served was primarily an affluent, upper middle class, large congregation, with many executives and business professionals who understood large organizations and the internal mechanics of organizational structures. The governance model and makeup might be described as a fast paced, stream lined, well-oiled machine. I likened it to a F-16 fighter jet, able to take off quickly, fly at supersonic speeds, do quick turns, barrel rolls, and fly to someone in need in no time at all. The governance model and mentality of the congregation was like that. Things usually moved quickly, were understood well, and freed workers to do what they loved to do. (That is probably a more idealistic picture than things really were, but for the analogy's sake it is accurate enough.)

When I arrived at Zion I made the mistake of assuming the governance and temperament of the congregation was the same as my previous congregation. Thus, as I tried to fly through expectations and strategic planning, I kept experiencing extreme turbulence. I was getting uncomfortable and frustrated. I wanted to take off at rocket speed, bank left or right as needed, hit supersonic speed, and get to those in need in no time at all. But it wasn't happening like I thought it should. I failed to first properly get to know my congregation—to love my congregation—and just assumed they would be like my last one. However, I failed to consider that the congregation was smaller and had a different history and mentality that was a mix of rural and farming, only recently adding suburbanites, having small town tendencies and customs that focused on relationships more than employing organizational tactics.

Where I was flying an F-16, they were flying a Cessna 172 (a single piston-engine, four-seat aircraft in production since the 1950s). At first, I thought I could just pull up, drop back from my supersonic speeds, come alongside of the Cessna, and then get her to blast into high speed with me once she caught sight of me. But I was badly mistaken and only found myself flying solo for the first number of years and wasting a lot of fuel. Finally, I realized I needed to repent of my stubbornness and land, get out of the F-16, put it in the hanger and go get to know the joys of the Cessna 172, becoming intimately familiar with how she flies and what she can do. I had to take the time to get to know my congregation and love them for who they were, how they thought about things, how they interacted with one another as an organization, and only then begin implementing a strategic plan at the speeds and altitudes they were comfortable with.

Lest you find yourself flying solo, get to know the way your congregation thinks and acts. Find out what kind of plane she is flying before you begin implementing a strategic plan.

THE BIG PICTURE: MISSION, VISION, STRATEGY, AND TACTICS

Once these issues are understood, an overall big picture can begin to be mentally or strategically generated by the pastor in conjunction with his staff or church lay leaders. Think of it like a zoomed-out picture of the whole ministry of your congregation and her workers. When that picture is mentally captured (or perhaps mapped out in diagrams and charts) then, like on a smart phone, you can zoom in on one portion of it at a time to see what it looks like, or what you might desire it to look like and sound like. As you identify those desires, you can then begin to make elements of a strategic plan that would move your congregation, or your fellow workers, toward any one specific goal.

Of course, these goals need to be clearly thought out, specific, measurable, attainable, realistic, and time certain. They need to be SMART: Specific, Measurable, Attainable, Realistic, Timely. There are numerous templates that can be used to create and track SMART goals. These can be used by staff members, or boards, committees, or ministry action teams. The point of them is not to create them for the sake of creating them, but to utilize them in moving the congregation or staff toward the desired and agreed upon goal.

But once the big picture is established, and various desires have been identified, a strategic plan can begin to be created.

Again, the use of a strategic plan is simply and only to serve the already identified theology and mission of the church as expressed in the Scriptures, but as applied to your specific time and setting. Strategic plans never supplant God's plan; they apply his plan to your situation. There are multiple ways of developing a strategic plan, some of them extremely expensive and wasteful. My congregation found that out the hard way.

Two years prior to my arrival, a strategic planning guru had been brought in (for a whopping $20,000) to help the congregation establish goals and objectives and move them on to what he said was their mission. When I arrived, no one in the congregation could actually articulate to me what the congregation's mission was based upon that consultant's work. They could only point me to the 10-page document he generated for them, at what amounted to $2,000 a page.

Perhaps you can understand, then, why I decided to finally take on creating a strategic plan myself for the congregation, a plan still utilized by the congregation some ten years later. (See the "Strategic Planning" diagram.) My point is that discernment and good judgment must be used regarding whether or not to employ professionals that will ask a lot of money from you, and very often simply give you a pre-made plan that may or may not work for your congregation, staff, or ministry focus.

BASICS OF STRATEGIC PLANNING

The basic elements of a strategic plan are meant to help your congregation identify the following:

- A mission (simplified statement of your congregation's purpose: who you are)

- A vision (what that mission looks like in the life of people and congregation: why it matters)

- A strategy (how the mission will be done)

- Tactics (the specific tools that will be employed).

Depending on the size and savvy of your congregation and workers, simpler might be better. Sometimes strategic plans only end up serving to make us busy without ever accomplishing anything except to generate a lot of PowerPoint shows or put a bunch of organizational buzz words on paper that may make us look smart but really have no impact on the organizational aspect of the congregation. Understanding the strategic planning process is important, but even more important is knowing why you want to utilize the process at your local congregation, and who should be involved in it.

If you want to pursue the specifics and details of how to create a strategic plan you can consult any number of books written specifically for crafting such plans for nonprofit organizations, though it is not necessary to do so. Remember that this is not your primary purpose as a pastor. If you find yourself spending more time researching

Mission:

Sharing hope and
teaching Christ
through word and
sacrament and
liturgical living.

Vision:

Being disciples by
following Jesus Christ
to the poor, the meek,
the destitute, the
lonely, the burdened,
the sick, sinners,
the cross, and
the empty tomb.

Strategic Planning

Zion Lutheran Church
(Mayer, MN)

Strategy:

Be the royal
priesthood by
sharing what we
have been given to
share through cradle-
to-grave Christian
education (1 Pet 2:9).

Tactics:

— Caring conversations
— Rituals & traditions
— Devotions
— Service

ZION LUTHERAN CHURCH — MAYER, MN

Word & sacrament
liturgical worship

Sharing the faith

Mission Statement:
Living the faith
in the world

Serving through our vocations

how to create a strategic plan than you do writing a sermon, praying, or visiting people, you likely have your priorities out of alignment.

CONCLUSION

So, there you have it: some simple ways to think about what it means to be a leader as you go about developing your pastoral *habitus*. In my own case, I learned many things the hard way. I cannot, of course, prevent you from learning that way too, but I hope at least I've pointed out some of the pitfalls for you. Perhaps I have offered some resources to help you avoid the many misbeliefs of self-reliance and leadership idolatry, as well as the headaches of making things more difficult than they really have to be.

In the end, the church is and always will be the Lord's church. No matter how great or poor a leader you or I may be, we can rejoice that the success of the church will always be based upon the shed blood of Jesus Christ and his victory over sin, death, and the power of the devil, and not our prowess as a leader. Yes, there is great joy in simply being a servant of the Lord's people, or as my dear friend Pastor Senkbeil so wonderfully says it, a sheepdog for Jesus. God bless you as you serve.

CHAPTER **3**

Leading Your Sheep—Administration and Strategic Planning

(Harold L. Senkbeil)

Every group needs a leader, or else they wander off in all directions at once. So you don't have a choice as to whether you are going to be a leader. The only question is what kind of leader you are. Are you going to get out ahead of your people and lead them? Or will you be wasting a lot of energy scurrying around to round them up? Take your cue from Jesus; he believes in leading more than chasing. Here's how he describes the work of a shepherd:

> The sheep hear his voice, and he calls his own sheep by name and leads them out. When he has brought out all his own, he goes before them, and the sheep follow him, for they know his voice. A stranger they will not follow, but they will flee from him, for they do not know the voice of strangers. (John 10:3–5)

Jesus, our Great Shepherd, calls his sheep one by one, leads them out into his flock, then gets out ahead of them all. And they follow along behind him because they know his voice. He speaks with a compelling combination of love and authority.

So as a pastor I'd suggest you follow Jesus' lead: Compassionately chase down sinners with God's law, but always lead them by his gospel.

It's never either/or; it's always both/and. That's what Jesus does, and that's what you do too since you are doing his work. He has appointed you to your office and authorized you to do what he's given you to do. Like Jesus, get out in front of your sheep; don't hang back in the shadows.

SPEAK UP

Instead, speak up in his name and stead. Use your voice to speak the words he's authorized you to speak: words of forgiveness, life, and peace through Jesus' blood and righteousness; words of comfort, hope, and consolation in the presence and power of his Holy Spirit; words of cleansing, renewal, and sanctification by means of his shared holiness. When you do that, the people you've been called to serve will in a very real way hear the voice of Jesus. And when they do, they will respond, again, not so much to you as to him.

Don't let this go to your head, though. Since the sheep and lambs of Jesus respond to him, don't think of yourself more highly than you ought to think (Rom 12:3). You've got nothing to give you have not first received. So don't get up on your high horse and bully people into doing what you think they should do. Don't be so full of yourself that you get in the way of people seeing Jesus. He must increase. You, on the other hand, must decrease. That works reciprocally; the more Jesus they see in you, the less obvious you become. Yet there's a strange paradox at work here as well. As you deliberately defer to Jesus, diminishing the role of your own personality, the more effective your ministry becomes. As you relinquish your personal authority, exalting his, the more authority you gain in people's eyes.

POWER VS. AUTHORITY

This is what I call the principle of power vs. authority. Depending on the English version you use, you can sometimes find these words used interchangeably in the New Testament. That's because only one word lies behind both in the original language: *exousia*. The Bible, however, makes a clear distinction between authorized power and unauthorized power. The only legitimate way to do ministry is by way of the authority of Jesus: doing what he's given you to do. Step out of the chain of his authority and you're on your own. And that's when things go south in a hurry.

In this chapter I'll use the word "authority" for power authorized by Jesus (to preach the gospel, to comfort the grieving, to call sinners to repentance, etc.) and the word "power" for unauthorized power (a directive originating not in Jesus but in the personal preferences of the pastor).

Many unfortunate dysfunctions arise when power is confused with authority. When pastors operate not out of their divinely commissioned authority but rather out of their private opinions and desires, conflict usually occurs. Likewise when congregations exert pressure on their pastors to conform to their own desires rather than defer to God's word, conflict and spiritual mayhem is the result.

Limited power

That's because power is a finite commodity. Within any group of people there's a limited amount of power. It is the sum total of the power of every individual in the group. One powerful personality can successfully impose his own will on the group, but he can only do that by taking power away from other people. As you can imagine, they're usually not too happy about this arrangement. This power equation, you might call it, adds to the pastor's power by taking it away from the people he serves. So when a pastor leads with power, he's creating a power imbalance. By asserting himself, he's robbing people of their power.

This works for a while; it may even work for quite a while, depending on the strength of the pastor's personality. But you can see that it's a strategy fraught with danger. It breeds resentment and discontent within a congregation for sure, and often these situations get ugly. People may suffer silently for a while, but eventually their resentment spills over into open resistance and rebellion. Now you've got a power struggle and contest of wills on your hands, as the pastor keeps trying to outsmart the opposition and form allegiances among his fans against his enemies. It's a powder keg situation politically speaking. And you know for sure you're in for trouble when the church is viewed increasingly from a political point of view.

So when you do ministry by power you've got a potential brouhaha on your hands organizationally speaking. Worst of all, where pastor and people lock horns in a political power struggle a church is collectively delivered into the hands of the great politician, the great power broker: Satan.

Unlimited authority

Authority is quite another matter. That's because authority does not originate in the human will, but in God himself. His mercies are new every day, and his compassion knows no bounds. His eternal life and love flow from his infinite nature, for even before the world began, from everlasting to everlasting he is God. He is not merely the source of love, but he is love in himself (1 John 4:8). So as God himself is limitless, his authority is likewise unlimited.

This has profound implications for pastoral leadership. Lead with power and you'll eventually run into a roadblock. Lead with authority, on the other hand, and you always have a future. Authority never runs out. As Christ's called and ordained servant, the more you exercise his authority, the more authority you have in people's estimation. As they perceive you are acting on behalf of Jesus and bringing his gifts, they defer more and more to your spiritual leadership.

When you do the bidding of Jesus, you never run out of resources for ministry. If you try to make things happen out of your own willpower and adrenalin, you'll crash and burn in a hurry. Effective sheepdogs derive their energy from the shepherd they serve. A good sheepdog never barks or bites, he just goes happily on carrying out the shepherd's directives. Even when he can't see the results himself, that dog is confident that the shepherd knows what he's doing and has things well in hand. So he's content to keep on keeping on, completely delighted to do his master's will.

LEADING AS SERVICE

You might detect a potential contradiction here. How can you get out ahead of your people as a leader and yet not impose your own will on people? Aren't these concepts mutually contradictory? Not really. Genuine authority in the church is always delegated. When you assume leadership as a pastor you don't take the lead; Jesus does. You accomplish your work as an authorized servant of the word, not a tyrant imposing your own will on the people of your flock.

To the casual observer, and quite possibly to a good share of your congregation, this style of leadership could make you seem weak. In our take-charge, can-do world in which powerful personalities make a big impact, someone who takes the lead with delegated authority might appear weak and ineffective. But that's not the case according to Jesus:

> A dispute also arose among them, as to which of them was to be regarded as the greatest. And he said to them, "The kings of the Gentiles exercise lordship over them, and those in authority over them are called benefactors. But not so with you. Rather, let the greatest among you become as the youngest, and the leader as one who serves. For who is the greater, one who reclines at table or one who serves? Is it not the one who reclines at table? But I am among you as the one who serves." (Luke 22:24–27)

The kingdom of God operates differently than human society. In his economy, it's not those who are being served who are the most important, but those who serve. By God's own design, servant leaders are on the bottom of the heap, not the top. In giving we receive, in losing we gain. And of course ultimately, in dying we live. That's not humanity's way. But it most certainly is God's way.

Christ-like servanthood includes emptying oneself, setting aside your own self-interests and deferring to the needs of others. This attitude Paul calls the "mind of Christ" (Phil 2:5). And all those who by baptism into Christ have crucified the desires of their sinful nature and put on Christ himself have this very mind in themselves. This is the outlook or attitude with which faithful pastors approach their work, and I commend this approach to you. You needn't ask, "What would Jesus do?" because you are baptized into him and by faith he lives within you. The life you live in your body you live by faith in the Son of God who loved you and gave himself for you (Gal 2:20).

So take your cue from Jesus, who loved you all the way to death and back. Be willing and eager to set aside your own selfish ambitions for his sake. Pay attention to the needs of his sheep and lambs to meet their needs with the gifts of his redeeming love, which you dispense in his name and stead by means of his word and sacraments. Lead from the back seat.

Here's how it works when you lead from the back seat. I've been in situations where people—usually men, of course—push the envelope, testing my patience by questioning my judgment or authority. Their intent is clearly to make this a personal matter; they want to go *mano a mano*. My instinct is to push back to show them who's boss. But ministry is not about me but about the One who sent me. I've discovered it's best to take a breath, step back for a moment, and then step forward in quiet, confident assertion. "Let's take another look at this," I might say. "What does our Lord have to tell us about this in his word?" It's risky. Others may consider you weak, but you are actually strong in Christ when you have nothing to offer other than what he has given you. You will do great things in Jesus' name, but those things are what he does in you and through you, not what you spin out of your own mind or willpower.

ADMINISTRATION AND MINISTRY

You can't really be an effective pastor without being efficient in management procedures. During my thirty-one years of parish ministry, my circumstances varied widely: small town, campus ministry, mission planter, and a larger suburban parish. I found the percentage of time and degree of organization devoted to administration varied in each location. But the one constant was that all of them needed attention to parish management and administration.

There are plenty of resources available to you regarding efficient church office procedures. I'm not going into detail here, other than to stress this one point: you cannot ignore—still less, despise—administration and still be an effective pastor. But administration always serves ministry, not the other way around. Parish administration supports ministry in Jesus' name. The gifts of Christ are always distributed not by management strategies but by the means of his Holy Spirit: the gospel and the sacraments. The church as a spiritual fellowship is constituted spiritually, not managerially.

Yet efficient management procedures are as important to your church as they are to your household. Somebody has to take out the garbage at your house; someone needs to plan the menus and write the grocery list. A calendar and event planning are essential in the life of every family. Budgets and careful financial management help avoid fiscal chaos for the household and living within your means facilitates financial peace and stability at your house. Why should it be any different in the church? When planning and administration is neglected, the ministry of God's word and sacrament suffers.

A periodic systematic review of policies and procedures at your church will serve you well. That way all your volunteers can go about their work with both confidence and satisfaction. For instance, who's responsible for communications in both print and electronic media? What financial checks and balances are in place? How are offerings processed, and who handles payment of congregation obligations? Who is responsible for maintenance and repair of buildings and property? Who manages the events calendar? How are pastoral visits scheduled and reported? You get the idea. The list is almost endless. And yet not one of these areas is at the heart of the ministry. These management procedures are not essential for the church; yet they certainly are helpful. If any one of these areas failed, the Holy Spirit would still go on calling, gathering, and enlightening his church on earth. Yet careful attention to these areas clearly frees a pastor to do his work more intentionally.

THEN AND NOW

Change is inevitable with every passing era. Today the farm implements we used back in the 50's are found only in agriculture museums. For example, my dad raised corn on his one hundred sixty acre farm using a two-row planter. Now my brothers-in-law plant corn on thousands of acres with a thirty-six-row planter. Even so, my brothers-in-law and their sons share the same farmer *habitus*—the character and temperament crafted by patterns of work and life—I saw in my dad all those long years ago. They have the same innate love for farming and knowledge of sun, soil, and climate that characterized my father's generation and his father and grandfather before him. Only the methods—and the scale—are different.

It's the same when it comes to office procedures in the church; things have shifted radically. I'd never be able to use the same methods and tools for parish administration today that I used forty-eight years ago. In my first parish there was no secretary; I produced every Sunday church bulletin and newsletter personally using an old-fashioned typewriter and mimeograph machine. Those days are long gone now. Computer technology and laser or inkjet printers have come onto the scene. And as frustrating as learning new software can be, there's no way I would dream of going back to the old ways of managing my daily routine and work.

The classic *habitus* of the care of souls can be supported just as well by recent management tools as it was back in those early days of my ministry, or in the days of quill pens and inkwells, for that matter. There's just one ministry our Lord has given his church, and it's up to each generation in turn to take up this divine calling: gathering, feeding, and tending the sheep and lambs of Jesus he entrusted into the care of his servants in every era. Management tools and strategies change radically over the years, but the *habitus* is ever the same. It's rooted deep in every pastor's heart and soul. What he does flows from who he is: a sheepdog for the Great Shepherd.

Thus faithful pastors should aspire to quality leadership simply because they have an inner drive to be effective shepherds. Leading and shepherding go together. But the perennial question is this: what are you going to be leading with? If your leadership style comes from a power structure mode instead of the authority model, you'll look pretty much like any other CEO in corporate America, only with a spiritual product. So be sure to let your management style flow from your pastoral *habitus*; don't take off your pastoral hat when you tackle parish administration issues. In fact, I would say you should be deliberately thinking about how your administrative and management responsibilities enhance the work of the care of souls in your congregation. Review any existing procedures or policy manuals with two questions uppermost in your mind:

1. Do these stated policies enhance or hamper the care of souls in this place?

2. Does what we do in this place highlight or obscure what God is doing here by means of his word and sacrament?

MANAGEMENT AND MINISTRY

There's no getting around it: There will be management dimensions to every ministry, no matter how simple or complex it is. Even the disciples of Jesus had a money manager, for example. The apostles in Jerusalem appointed deacons to tend to the administrative details of the daily life of the Christian congregation. Management is a given. Logistical matters may be mundane in comparison to the central life and ministry of Christ's church, but they need attention. They remain peripheral to the heart and center of the church's life and being, but they are beneficial. Though they are helpful, they are not central. You can serve the Lord of the church and receive his gifts without budgets, print and media resources, calendars, and time management, but in our historical setting you can't do it well.

I've known men who are, to quote the proverb, "so heavenly minded they are of no earthly good," pastorally speaking. They focus on spiritual matters and ignore everything else. They wouldn't know an agenda or a financial report if it bit them. Their people skills are minuscule. They haven't the foggiest idea of how to recruit and manage volunteers or develop a system to stay in communication with a far-flung parish. They're too busy reading, researching, and thinking deep theological thoughts to get much of anything done beyond preaching and occasional shut-in and hospital visits. Then again, they may get sucked into the black hole of Internet debate via blog posts and social media exchanges, lobbing volleys back and forth in theological jousting matches rather than visiting and caring for the souls for whom Jesus bled and died.

On the other hand, I've known others who—though they bear the title of pastor—act more like corporate executives than shepherds of souls. Their days are so jammed with administrative tasks that there's precious little time left over for anything else. Some of them even relegate the care of souls to laity. Not to disparage caring Christians and the loving support and care they can give, but when you're crashing and burning spiritually speaking, you don't need first aid or a paramedic or even a nurse practitioner. You need a fully trained, licensed, and experienced physician. So please don't relinquish your sacred calling; don't turn over the cure of souls for whom Jesus died to novices.

So my advice is this: Keep a finely tuned balance of both informed administration and intentional ministry. Make sure that essential things remain up front and central, but don't neglect helpful things that free you for intelligent and dedicated ministry as a servant of Christ and steward of God's mysteries. You will find, as I have, that you can tend to secondary matters without neglecting the primary.

FROM SIMPLE TO COMPLEX

I already told you that in my first parish I handled not only the care of souls, but all the support services as well. It was a great help in succeeding locations to have some clerical assistance. In the mission congregation I served, church meetings, midweek services, and youth instruction happened in the family room on the lower level of our home. Once each week a volunteer came over and did the printing for Sunday morning on a donated mimeograph machine. Leaders at that mission told me early on I needed to focus on preaching and the word of God while they provided these essential volunteer services.

Some years later I was called to a large suburban parish with a Christian day school, a full complement of classroom teachers, principal, youth worker, two pastors, three administrative assistants and a parish administrator. I went the full gamut from serving a flock that could fit in my living room to one that filled a large sanctuary twice over on a Sunday morning. I can confidently tell you that no matter how simple or complex the setting, the challenge always remained the same: to keep the main thing the main thing, to not allow the tail to wag the dog, to keep the focus on the divine means of the Holy Spirit by which alone the church is built and nourished: the gospel and sacraments.

I can also confidently tell you that the degree of attention and planning involved in management/administration expands with the size of the church. This can easily intrude on both the quantity and quality of your distinctly pastoral duties. Savvy and spiritually mature lay leadership can help evaluate the need for support staff to ensure that, just as in the Jerusalem congregation, those who serve in Jesus' name don't set aside prayer and the ministry of the word to wait on tables. Ministry and administration belong together. Yet they are not interchangeable; the latter serves the former. Don't get this mixed up and set aside the one thing needful to be busy and preoccupied with many other things. Only the ministry of the gospel and sacrament feeds and nourishes Christ's flock and cares for their souls; this and this alone remains primary. Everything else, as helpful as it might be, is secondary. But it takes planning to keep your priorities in order.

WHAT'S YOUR PLAN?

You know that planning is involved in every human venture. From managing your household calendar to going on a family vacation, it all takes a certain amount of planning. The more people involved and the more complex the project, the more planning is needed. This is just common sense.

Now hear me clearly on this. I'm not implying that you can make your church grow through the planning process. The operative power for the church's life—whether in evangelization or the care of souls—always remains the Holy Spirit working through his means. In my dad's farming operation he knew that the operative force in his crop or animal production was not based on his strategies, planning, management, or hard work. Horticulture and animal husbandry are rooted in the forces of God the Father's creative power; a combination of the plant and animal genetics built into his creation and nurtured by sun, soil, and water. In a very real sense my father was merely a manager of God's good creation. He didn't cause the growth; he merely managed it. But he worked vigorously to manage it well.

I think that's the posture you and I need when it comes to leadership, administration, and planning as pastors. We're not the creators; we're only the managers. We can't cause the growth or success of our congregation or ministry any more than my dad could produce a corn crop or raise quality beef, pork, or chickens. He simply managed what God created. So do we. The church is God's own creation, the holy bride of Christ created and nurtured by the blood and water that flowed from his crucified side. You and I as servants of Christ and stewards of God's mysteries merely manage his good gifts in order to faithfully serve the sheep and lambs of Jesus and to gather his other sheep into his fold now and eternally.

ROW BOATS AND CRUISE SHIPS

Keep in mind that as larger churches need more planning, they also need more lead time. When our little mission congregation was planted, the lay leaders and I could strategize our plans rather quickly. But when it began to grow in numbers, we needed more advance planning. Later when I served the large suburban parish, not only was the administration more complex, but plans had to be put in place long before they were executed. The goal of planning was the same, but the process was different. Both churches had a destination in mind; it's just that the larger church needed more time to achieve the goal.

I liken this distinction to be very much like the difference between steering a rowboat and a cruise ship. A little boat can turn fairly quickly; a large ship needs slight adjustments to her course well in advance so that the final destination can be achieved with minimal impact on contents and passengers. In both situations establishing a clear destination comes first, but in the second case more strategizing will be necessary.

STRATEGIC PLANNING

If you take your office and calling seriously you'll want to look not only at the immediate needs of your flock, but their long range welfare as well. Together with the leadership of your church you'll want to lay out a long term strategy that informs the allocation of your collective resources (both people and funding) as you move ahead together in service of the Lord's mission.

This is where strategic planning comes in. A strategy is extremely helpful. Notice that adjective; I said helpful. We need to distinguish what's essential from what's helpful. What's essential for the future of Christ's church is what is central in every era: the calling, gathering, and enlightening of the Holy Spirit through the gospel and sacraments. Every church needs a pastor, in other words. People can't believe without hearing, and they can't hear without a preacher, and preachers can't preach unless they are sent (Rom 10:14–15). So a church can live without a strategy; but it lives much better when it charts out its priorities and directions.

It's possible that some of you have had some experience in business and industry and have been exposed to various strategic planning processes. But most clergy have had no training and little or no experience in that area. I'd suggest that you consult with some spiritually mature corporate leaders in your church to get a better perspective on the process. Read a couple of the better secular books on strategic planning to gain more insights. (Have a look at Lucas Woodford's overview of books on strategic planning for churches in chapter 2). Then sit down together with a few key leaders in your church and design a process that would best serve your circumstances. The best strategic plans set a limited number of goals for the immediate and near future, which can then guide you in the allocation of time, energy, and finances as you move along from year to year. This provides continuity and direction as opportunities arise; each can be evaluated as to how well it fits into the overall strategic plan.

In most strategic planning processes you'll run across the terms "values" and "vision." Don't be put off by them. True, they could be abused if someone assumes that the pastor is the equivalent of an executive in a large corporation whose job as a visionary leader is to enlist senior management to sign on to his personal goals and organize the business around his personal priorities. Yet the simple reality is that every enterprise from the most mundane to the most ethereal has shared values and a central vision. No army can defend its citizenry and defeat its enemy if it goes off in all directions at once. Every military operation needs a well defined strategic initiative and objective as well as clearly articulated tactics designed to achieve that objective.

Strategic planning in the church is abused when more time and energy is invested the planning process than in actual ministry. But it's equally tragic when there's no plan at all. Unspoken or inarticulate objectives give leaders the impression that the church has no vision or purpose beyond external institutional survival. Notice that our Lord Jesus spelled out the objective and strategy for his disciples' apostolic ministry:

> Jesus said to them again, "Peace be with you. As the Father has sent me, even so I am sending you." And when he had said this, he breathed on them and said to them, "Receive the Holy Spirit. If you forgive the sins of any, they are forgiven them; if you withhold forgiveness from any, it is withheld." (John 20:21–23)

In a nutshell, my position on leadership, parish administration, and strategic planning is this: when secondary matters take priority, the ministry suffers. But likewise ministry suffers when secondary matters are neglected and everyone fends for themselves organizationally speaking. Below I've provided eight benchmarks for faithful and effective strategic planning. Note that the first (and most important) benchmark is the presence of the living Lord with his church and faithfulness to his written word. When Scripture casts the strategic vision and informs the tactics, the stage is set for cohesive and effective ministry.

I asked my dear friend and colleague Lucas Woodford to write a guide on administration and planning because he knows the literature. Not only is he much better read in the planning processes than I am, but he's "been there and done that" when it comes to strategic planning. And as you can tell from the first chapter in this book he knows where the landmines lie. Combine his experience and knowledge with the spiritual principles I outline below, and you'll find a winning combination for parish administration and planning.

STRATEGIC PLANNING DESIGN

We can borrow certain elements of the secular planning process for church planning. But there are distinct differences between the two. First of all, the church is not a business, the gospel is not a product, and the ministers of Christ are not salesmen. That means customers aren't kings, as they are in the corporate business world. Not that people for whom Jesus died are customers for the gospel, far from it. They are always recipients of his saving grace. Yet their desires and felt needs never determine the content and shape of the church's mission and ministry. The mission of the church is always defined by Christ Jesus, and her ministry is designed by him.

That's where to begin, then, with these four basic assumptions: (1) Faithful proclamation of the gospel and administration of the sacraments are the only means by which the church grows and prospers. (2) The Scriptures are the sole source and norm of all teaching in the church. (3) The context of the mission does not position its shape and content, rather the text of the Scriptures positions the mission in any given context. (4) We must faithfully engage each contemporary culture, yet our task is to acculturate people into the church's transcendent culture.

Here are eight steps in preparing for an effective strategic planning design:

FIRST: Real Presence

As the Lord Jesus sent his apostles into all the world to make disciples of all nations, baptizing them in the name of Father, Son, and Holy Spirit and teaching them to observe all that he had commanded them, he reminded them they would never be alone: "And behold, I am with you always, to the end of the age" (Matt 28:20).

When church-related entities set about the strategic planning process this promise is too often set aside. In effect, Christians then become functional agnostics. When a church's strategic planning process clouds the gospel it's bad enough, but when it assumes the gospel it's even worse. Then you end up with a strategy that looks just like another secular fund appeal with some Bible passages thrown in.

When, on the other hand, the living presence of the living Christ by means of his gospel preached and sacraments administered is the throbbing heart of the entire process from the initial steps to the desired outcomes, it transforms the whole procedure. Then you have a truly Christ-centered process and churchly plan. So ultimately this first component informs every other step along the way.

Ask:

- Is Christ Jesus and him crucified, risen, and ascended the heart and center of our church's life and mission?

- How is that articulated and demonstrated in our planning process?

- How can we best ensure that all our people rely on Christ's continuing presence through his gospel and sacraments for addressing and meeting the challenges before us?

SECOND: Who are we?

It would be tragic to outline a plan for the future that takes us off course. So we need to start at the beginning, defining our values and vision. Likewise, we can't very well set goals for our future together if we don't know where we've come from.

Ask:

- Who are we?

- What mutual beliefs and values do we have as the people of God in this place who share a common confession of the faith once delivered to the saints? (Jude 1:3)

- What have been some key events in our congregation's history? What is our shared experience?

- What shifts in demographics or ethnicities have changed our community profile and impact our church's current ministry in this place?

- What new mission are we being called to in this location? How does that refocus our priorities?[6]

THIRD: What resources do we have?

When our Lord asked his disciples where they would buy bread to feed the crowd by the Sea of Tiberias, they began with an inventory. Philip said that two hundred days' wages wouldn't be enough, and they didn't have that much cash. But Andrew pointed out that a small boy in the crowd had on hand five loaves and two fish (John 6:1–14). You know of course that Jesus started with those meager resources and then multiplied them to feed five thousand men, plus women and children. So it's good to take careful stock of what Jesus has to work with in our congregation.

Ask:

- What aptitudes, skills, and vocations are represented among our members, leaders, and called workers?

- How can these best be mobilized in volunteer and compensated service to our Lord and his mission?

- What material and financial resources have our people been blessed with from which gifts can be directed to advance the Lord's work in this place?

FOURTH: Profile

As the gospel had its way among the members of the first congregation in Jerusalem, Luke records that those first Christians had "favor among all the people" (Acts 2:47). Through their normal interaction with their neighbors, the word of the Lord grew and the Lord added to their number daily those who were being saved. It's good to know how our current members fit within our community.

Ask:

- What are the demographics of our current membership in comparison with our surrounding community?

- How does the socio-economic makeup of our congregation compare with our neighbors?

- Most importantly, what links do we already have to our community?

- Where are the natural bridges for caring conversations with other people who may not yet know the Lord Jesus?

FIFTH: Cultural Challenges

In every era there are collective assumptions of society that place roadblocks and obstacles in the way of Christian faith and life. It's important that these are periodically reviewed and identified, or they may influence our collective confession and shared values. Paul wrote to the Christians in Rome that they were not to "conform to this world" (Rom 12:2). One paraphrase of this text puts it more vividly: "Don't let the world around you squeeze you into its own mold."[7] So it's good to routinely and regularly take an honest and objective look at the setting of our mission spiritually and socially.

Ask:

- What spiritual, ethical, and sexual assumptions in our culture challenge our clear confession of the biblical gospel?

- What Christian teachings will we need to emphasize in order to counter these challenges and create a church climate designed to welcome in refugees from a world in moral and spiritual collapse?

- How can we best equip our members to raise their children to live confidently and faithfully in the years ahead?

SIXTH: Staffing

People are always more important than real estate. Starting in late antiquity, through the middle ages and into the modern era, Christians have tended to think of the church in terms of brick and mortar. Yet these buildings are not important in themselves, but because of what happens there as the gospel is preached and the sacraments are administered. In fact, because of looming persecution the day may not be far off when churches will not be able to maintain the elaborate buildings we in the West have taken for granted for centuries. So in order to plan strategically, congregations should spotlight the most important component in their life and mission: the support of the people who staff Christ's ministry among them. "In the same way, the Lord commanded that those who proclaim the gospel should get their living by the gospel" (1 Cor 9:14). A good strategic plan will provide for the pastoral office and needed personnel that support pastoral work in the midst of the congregation.

Ask:

- What called workers, including the pastor, are necessary to proclaim Christ and his word, care for the souls of our congregation, reach the lost, and equip our children and adults to meet the unique challenges of our generation over the next three to seven years?

- What support staff would help our our called workers fulfill their responsibilities among us?

- What volunteers from our membership will we need to recruit, train, and coordinate to best enable our called workers and support staff to serve joyfully and effectively in this place?

SEVENTH: Capital Needs

All too frequently strategic plans are driven by building projects. There's nothing wrong with financing buildings, of course, but you'll notice that this item comes seventh in my list of priorities. Buildings are secondary to people; I submit that you can't objectively address building needs apart from ministry goals. Without a clearly articulated ministry plan, building projects devolve into fund raising. On the other hand, when people capture the vision of what the church is and what her mission is—once they see the centrality of the gospel and its proclamation in their corporate life—then they are all the more motivated to support this helpful (but non-essential) aspect of the church's mission.

Ask:

- What capital needs does our church have in order to support the mission we have outlined above? (Consider the maintenance and expansion of existing facilities as well as constructing new ones.)

- How can we ensure that our church building and property remain tools for mission and ministry rather than idolatrous impediments?

- How can we devise the best way to realistically assess our actual building needs (as opposed to wants) and collectively identify the best way to meet those needs?

EIGHTH: Financial Goals

Notice this item comes last. Too often churches put it first. Unfortunately what frequently drives churches into strategic planning is a financial crunch. And when that happens, the bottom line drives the process, thus effectively derailing the whole effort. Remember that the church's main activity is not fund raising, but ministry of word and sacrament. God doesn't need our gifts; he is already in possession of every beast in the forest and the cattle on a thousand hills (Ps 50:50). In a very real way people do not give anything to God, but rather return to him for his use a portion of what he has already given them. Every appeal for financial gifts, whether for operating or capital needs, needs to be founded on solid ministry goals, biblically based and clearly communicated.

Ask:

- What are our financial goals in order to support our workers and capital needs for the next three to five years?

- How will we organize a campaign biblically informed and rooted in our confession to educate, motivate and enlist the gifts necessary to meet those goals?

If you've been using these eight steps in devising your planning process, do me a favor. Before you go any further, review each of the steps (especially the last two) in light of the first. "Unless the Lord builds the house, those who build it labor in vain" (Ps 127:1). And the invisible presence of Jesus by means of his living word is at the heart of your church's vitality. "No one can lay a foundation other than that which is laid, which is Jesus Christ" (1 Cor 3:11).

CONCRETE PLANNING

The advantage of a good strategic plan is not only that it provides you with clear direction, but it also provides a standard of evaluation. This means when something doesn't fit within your adopted objectives it's likely undeserving of allocation of resources (both in terms of personnel or financials) and should be discarded. Strategic planning keeps you on target.

Quality strategic plans are always concrete, never abstract, designed for specific implementation in a specific setting.

CONTINGENCIES

My goal here has been to help you see how faithful ministry in Jesus' name drives every aspect of the church's life, including organization and managerial matters as well as strategic planning. Though in some respects strategic planning in the church leans on secular planning models, it breathes a different atmosphere and weaves a different tapestry. Its warp and woof is the life that Christ Jesus lives through all his saints, and the golden thread from which it's spun is his efficacious gospel.

But no matter how carefully and faithfully you plan, sometimes things don't turn out as you've planned. When that happens, it's good to go back to the beating heart of your plan and its desired outcomes: the living presence of the living Christ by means of his gospel preached and sacraments administered. Jesus Christ remains the Lord of the church, after all, and his continuing presence and promise sustains her life and mission in this world and her life to all eternity: "I will build my church, and the gates of hell will not prevail against it" (Matt 16:18).

A FAILED PLAN?

God's ways are not our ways, nor are our ways his. The most faithfully devised plan may not come to fruition. It's been that way since the days of the apostles. In Acts 16, for example, Luke records that Paul and his missionary colleagues had set out for Bithynia, a province in the northern region of Asia Minor (modern day Turkey). "But the Spirit of Jesus did not allow them" (v. 7). So they turned west, toward Troas. There Paul had a vision of a Macedonian man urging him to come to Greece to preach the gospel. The rest, as they say, is history. The foundation of the church in Corinth and the spread of the gospel in Athens and other parts of the Grecian peninsula resulted from what you might call a failed mission plan.

What exactly did it mean that "the Spirit of Jesus" did not permit Paul's best-laid plans to come to fruition? We don't really know, but many years ago a pastor whom I knew and respected suggested it might be that Paul got sick, for immediately after he records these incidents, Luke begins to write his record of Paul's missionary journeys in the first person plural. So Doctor Luke joined the missionary entourage at this point. Was it perhaps to care for an ailing Paul? We don't know this for a fact. But it's true that God the Holy Spirit guides and directs the mission of Christ's church according to his will, not ours. And when that happens, our plans need to be adjusted to conform to his.

So plan carefully, then, but in all your planning check your outcomes and goals against the Spirit's word. Pray for his guidance and presence, and entrust yourself and the whole process to his leading. He will bring it to completion in his own way and time, believe you me.

But watch yourself, so you don't fall into the trap that almost finished Pastor Woodford before he got started as a leader. There's a progression to the dysfunction he outlined in chapter one, and it can be avoided by the grace of God if you're alert to the symptoms.

CHAPTER 4

Pastoral Depletion Syndrome

(Harold L. Senkbeil)

In each succeeding generation, it seems that pastors are abandoning their vocations in ever increasing numbers. Some may chalk this up to rapidly shifting demographics and worldviews. And while it cannot be denied that in our post church culture tried-and-true methods come up dry—a very depleting scenario for anyone who seriously loves Jesus and his church—I'm convinced there's more to this phenomenon than shifting social metrics.

I believe the largest factor in the startling number of pastors who resign their calls or are driven from them by dysfunctional congregations is the loss of pastoral identity. Churches have forgotten what pastors are supposed to do, and we pastors just don't know who we are any more. And so we cast about looking for some role to play, like starving actors trying to land a job. The problem is that at every audition someone hands us a different script and we can never really get a handle on it. We have a hard time getting inside the character we're supposed to play, so we go about our role rather woodenly. We become pastoral mimics: pastor impersonators, you could say. We keep on trying extra hard but we get nowhere fast. When that sad cycle starts, pastors begin exhibiting serious symptoms of what I call the pastoral depletion syndrome.

Here's the usual progression. A young pastor (he doesn't have to be young, but it helps; when you're young you're looking to make your mark, gain approval, and please your people) moves through three stages on his way to depletion: confusion, desperation, then finally capitulation.

CONFUSION

What's a guy to do? There's so much to be done and so little time to do it in. There are so many people to serve and they're never all satisfied no matter how hard I work and what I try. How do I attract more people to this church and keep them interested? What can I give out that will leave them wanting to come back for more?

Imagine you're a young man like that who loves his Lord and wants to serve Christ's church. Imagine you've just graduated from a seminary where you've been handed a rich legacy out of the accumulated wisdom of the ages. You've got an above average grasp of the biblical languages and you've been carefully trained in how to weave a reasonably interesting and compelling sermon from the threads of the ancient texts of Scripture. You've got more than a nodding acquaintance with the church's history so you can trace the major movements of theological thought down through the centuries. You have been trained in the church's dogma and you can talk intelligently about the chief parts of Christian doctrine. You've acquired basic entry skills in evangelism, church administration, teaching, visitation. Still you feel ill equipped. Why?

Because nothing seems to work like you thought it would. You compare yourself with other more effective (shall we say successful?) pastors, and inside you begin to wonder whether you're cut out for this job. You are confused; you've done all you've been given to do and yet it never seems enough. You're able to please some of the people some of the time but you never seem to be able to please all the people all the time. And so slowly you begin to shrivel up and something dies inside. Despite doing your level best, your best is apparently not enough.

Do you get the picture? Can you see the impending danger looming? See how the stage is set for disaster? Something's gone radically wrong here. What is it?

One response is to become shopkeepers instead of servants of the living Lord. As Eugene Peterson says: "The pastors of America have metamorphosed into a company of shopkeepers, and the shops they keep are churches. They are preoccupied with shopkeeper's concerns—how to keep the customers happy, how to lure customers away from competitors down the street, how to package the goods so that the customers will lay out more money. The marketing strategies of the fast-food franchise occupy the waking minds of these entrepreneurs; while asleep they dream of the kind of success that will get the attention of journalists."[8]

That's how it is when you set up shop in the spiritual shopping mall that the contemporary religious scene in America has become. You actually come to believe that the whole enterprise of Christ's church rests on your shoulders. You become persuaded that if you just work long enough and hard enough and smart enough, the stars will align and things will come together just right; business will be booming before you know it. Spectacular and dramatic results seem just around the corner. But of course that's exactly the problem; rarely does that sort of growth happen. Jesus says, "I will build my church," and when he does, give him thanks. But don't be surprised if not much happens despite all your hard work to set up shop in the American religious shopping mall.

Many of you know what failure to thrive in the ministry feels like firsthand. No doubt you've seen other pastors shrivel up and die or work themselves into an emotional basket case. When you lose touch with your vocation you begin to detach from those you love most and best because you think you need to pour more energy into making things happen. You've become persuaded that the resources for effective ministry lie within you, that all your desires for Christ's church and kingdom can be achieved if you just work harder and smarter. If you've ever been down that road, you know how lonely it can get. You know that continual lump in the pit of your stomach, what it feels like when you long for affirmation and seemingly you get unrelenting scrutiny instead. Inwardly you teeter on a fine line somewhere between despair and rage. It's not pretty, it's not healthy, and it leads to a vicious cycle of defensive posturing and avoidance that isolates you even more from the very support you yearn for from trusted colleagues and loved ones.

If you haven't experienced this for yourself, chances are you've seen it in other pastors. You know what happens when men become obsessed with success and are persuaded that if they'd just try harder, the results they crave are possible. Sadly, all too often those desired outcomes remain tantalizingly just outside reach. When that happens, a man who's actually a very good pastor begins to lose his grip. He's moved beyond confusion into desperation, the second stage of the pastoral depletion syndrome.

DESPERATION

A desperate pastor is a danger to himself and the congregation he serves. Things aren't healthy when he's confused, but when he becomes desperate he verges on the dysfunctional. Clinical symptoms like anxiety and depression are not uncommon, but even more alarming is what happens to him spiritually. He becomes a sitting duck for the temptations of devil, world, and flesh. He's convinced himself that radical readjustment is essential just to survive, so he's willing to try pretty much anything that comes along that promises to give the statistical lift he's looking for in his ministry.

Biblical and doctrinal standards go out the window in a frantic attempt to turn things around. At first there's a tinge of guilt and shame at lowering his standards, but after a while he persuades himself that desperate times call for desperate measures. A certain spiritual numbness descends on him; it's like he's developed callouses on his soul. If his prayer life hasn't suffered already, it takes a nosedive now. He may turn to alcohol or other drugs for help. Some men try treating their spiritual apathy and inner pain with a sure-fire jolt of Internet porn. It promises quick relief, an instant escape from intolerable tension, but it leaves a boat load of guilt and shame in its wake, intensifying the pain and locking a man ever more tightly in his own lonely little prison cell of desperation.

Ministry for a desperate pastor degenerates into role-play; he becomes increasingly emotionally distant and detached from most every dimension of pastoral work, from preaching to counseling to visitation to parish leadership. It's like he can't go anywhere in public without putting on his game face. And that game face masks a world of hurt inside. He's utterly convinced that by putting on a brave face and gutting through by sheer force and determination he can turn things around.

But ministry by adrenalin is no substitute for the real thing. It can come seductively close. It can approximate ministry, it can imitate ministry, perhaps it can even impersonate ministry, but it can't really sustain ministry for any length of time. Adrenalin is a finite commodity. Hard work will take you just so far before you run out of energy. Long hours take their toll physically and emotionally, to say nothing of what they do to family life. Personal resources can and must be brought into the service of God's kingdom, but they are not the source of kingdom growth. It's just as the prophet was instructed to tell governor Zerubbabel: "Not by might, nor by power, but by my Spirit, says the Lord of hosts" (Zech 4:6). The Spirit of God working through his word is the sole instrument of ministry, not hard work, intelligence, personal charm, nor strategic innovation and emotional energy.

You can get by with that approach for just so long—certainly a few months, perhaps even a few years. But sooner or later you're going to hit a wall. When you habitually do ministry out of your own resources, sooner or later you're going to run out. "Tapped out" are the words I hear frequently from bright and energetic pastors who've been attempting to do ministry out of the finite deposit of their own energy and intelligence. They're running on empty, and they can't sustain that very long. Something's got to give.

One of the first things to suffer is family life. Just ask the wife of any pastor who's reached the desperate stage: She has become effectively widowed. She begins feeling slighted by a man she thought loved her. Eventually she comes to resent the congregation that seems to attract so much of her husband's attention; if she's honest, she thinks of the church as the other woman in his life. And when children are deprived of their father's attention and love because he's in over his head in ministry, they, too, become resentful toward the church. Not uncommonly, they begin to harden their hearts toward a God they see as unrealistically demanding and unrelenting. They can see what's happening to their dad as he pours his heart into a ministry that saps his every ounce of energy and leaves him so exhausted physically and emotionally that he has nothing left over to give them.

Single men in ministry experience their own uniquely toxic form of desperation. Paradoxically, their singleness compounds the problem. Frequently the congregations they serve victimize and abuse them. Because he's got no wife or children who need him, they assume he should be on duty 24/7. Foolishly, single pastors occasionally buy into this delusion and become veritable Energizer bunnies in ministry. They try every trick in the book to meet the impossible expectations of an increasingly demanding church, all the while carelessly ignoring their own personal needs for rest and relaxation. When a man doesn't nourish his own soul by taking time for relaxation, recreation, and hobbies, his soul begins to shrivel. When he neglects cultivating and nourishing friendships, he lives alone in a sea of togetherness on an island of loneliness that grows smaller and smaller with every passing month. He may look busy on the outside, but meanwhile he's dying on the inside, leading a life of quiet desperation.

It's not a pretty picture. It's one I've seen far, far too many times over the years in pastors both married and single. I've fallen into this pitfall myself periodically. Still do, in fact. I'm continually tempted to set aside the needs of my wife and family and instead invest more time and energy into kingdom work. I'm old enough and experienced enough to know better, but there's still a compelling tug that deceives me into thinking that my real value is in my public reputation and what I achieve rather than in who I am and whose I am by baptism into Christ Jesus my Lord.

What makes us think we can run ministry out of the puny resources of our own mind and heart? Why do we set out to do the Lord's infinite work out of the finite capacity of our personal charisma and compassion? Most likely such foolishness can partially be explained by our ignorance. But when you get right down to it, this madness is largely misbelief. In reality we've turned a blind eye toward the promises of God in his word and the wondrous description he paints there of the nature of the church and her ministry. In the letter to the Ephesians the church is pictured as God's own household, built on the foundation of the apostles and prophets with Christ Jesus himself being the cornerstone (2:19–20). In his first letter to the Corinthians, Paul portrays himself and his colleagues as ministers of Christ and stewards of God's mysteries (4:1).

Yet these realities are equally invisible to ministers and the people they serve. Out of sight, out of mind. Invisible realities don't really register in human consciousness. Instead we tend to look for demonstrable methods that promise alluringly demonstrable results, given enough time and effort. Our Lord has given us a brain, and he expects us to use it in the service of his word. We are to love God with all our mind, as well as heart and soul and strength, says Jesus (Luke 10:27). There's nothing wrong with using rational, reasonable methods to support and extend ministry. Problems arise, however, when we rely on these rational methods and human brainpower and energy as the exclusive mode of ministry. When that happens, we begin to believe the lie that the Lord's work can actually be accomplished by human endeavor. So when things aren't getting done the way we would like, we work harder—usually with little to show for our efforts except more exhaustion and frustration. That's the inevitable result of misbelief's deception.

But ultimately the real culprit is pride. We're so damned arrogant (literally) that we think it's all about us. We create an idol made in our own image and likeness, the very definition of idolatry. That false god of self and adrenalin is relentless, and his demands are all consuming. We set out to become the envy of our peers in ministry and cultivate the admiration of those we serve in our congregation. We'd like to think that by our own reason and strength we can get the results we're looking for, so we redouble our efforts. More often than not, however, we end up with little to show for it except increased frustration bordering on exasperation.

That's the way it is when you turn your attention away from the limitless wellspring of God's love in Christ and tap into the puny little reservoir of your own ingenuity and adrenalin. When you keep running on empty, finally you run out.

Many a pastor knows what the tragic aftermath of desperation looks like: The holy things of God lose most of their appeal. There's little if any joy left in his daily routine. God's word and prayer are still there, but his heart isn't in it anymore. He can go through the motions, but finds little or no satisfaction in it. He feels like he's slogging through some never-ending swamp. Many resign at this stage.

If by sheer determination he's able to continue, he becomes adept at impersonating a pastor. When that happens, he moves into the third and final stage of pastoral depletion: capitulation.

CAPITULATION

Ironically, capitulation takes two forms. The first is obvious and predictable: The pastor just gives up. The second is subtler and more paradoxical: hyperactivity. Both are an immense personal tragedy and leave open wounds and scars on the body of Christ.

The first form of capitulation is all too familiar. The pastor realizes he's hit a wall or others realize it for him. The pain is too much to bear and he resigns his call or is forced to resign by his members or superiors. There are pressing concerns in those situations; how will he support himself and his family? What can he do with the rest of his life, given the fact that he's invested a tidy sum and some of the best years of his life getting the education and training required for the pastoral ministry? But the most pressing need of all often goes begging: his own profound spiritual hunger as well as a deep and abiding sense of failure. Too often a man who has given up or been forced out of the ministry is left to manage as best he can—referred to a therapist, maybe—a therapist he most likely can't afford. Rarely is he given spiritual attention by brothers in office or his superiors. He is the proverbial wounded solider left behind on the battlefield. Licking his wounds, he tries as best he can to come to terms with an abiding sense of being a wash-up, a vocational failure who just didn't have what it takes.

That's exactly right, but he doesn't realize the hidden wisdom beneath his profound sense of inability. The real reason he came up empty is that he had nothing inside to give. He's been completely tapped out. His ministry tank ran dry because he'd been going about ministry all wrong for far too long. He was trying to pastor others out of his own minuscule resources instead out of the limitless reservoir found in Christ Jesus and his gifts. And when you do that you're bound to run dry; it's inevitable.

Thankfully many of these men who resign their calls do receive responsible pastoral care for their sins—things they did wrong and things they left undone—but just as importantly, pastoral care for their hurts and wounds. Some don't, though, and this is a glaring scar on the body of Christ that needs a deliberate fix. From top on down everybody in the church needs to devote more loving attention to—and deliberate care for—these wounded warriors and their families. They should not be left to fend for themselves spiritually. Every level of the church needs to be engaged in addressing the spiritual needs of these men. God is surpassingly rich in his grace. There is abundant forgiveness in the shed blood of Jesus; there is lavish healing in his abiding love. There is divine strength in the Holy Spirit, the comforter who provides consolation and strength in his copious gifts through word and sacrament within the company of fellow sinner-saints in the church who shoulder each other's burdens and share each other's joys, weeping with those who weep and rejoicing with those who rejoice.

So healing is possible for those who have been defeated by the pastoral depletion syndrome. Capitulation can be treated in this case comparatively directly; recovery and healing is possible for those pastors who give up on ministry.

HYPERACTIVITY

But what happens when a man doesn't give up, but turns to hyperactive ministry instead, in a vain attempt to justify himself? That kind of capitulation in office is a much tougher nut to crack. Instead of throwing in the towel, a man resolves to stick with it. Remember, he's already disillusioned and desperate. That means that when he capitulates on faithful ministry by turning to hyperactivity there's an exponentially greater potential for spiritual mayhem and disaster.

His problem is largely invisible to the external observer. He's still there much as he always has been. Yet he's not there; not really. Inwardly something has died. He can still be observed doing the work of a pastor, but the *pastor* isn't there anymore. He has long since checked out of his work emotionally and spiritually. He's lost his *habitus*—and become merely habitual instead. He's traded shepherding for shop keeping and with a sigh of relief. Shop keeping comes natural to him because he's lost his true pastoral heart as a shepherd of souls. He knows his trade but he's abandoned his craft. He knows how to keep his demons at bay by maintaining an outward appearance of success, so he redoubles his efforts to be more successful. So he may look busy, busier than ever in fact. Yet all that busyness masks a deep spiritual void inside and provides a toehold for Satan, the father of lies.

For a hyperactive pastor his bottom line for pastoral work is measured increasingly by external standards rather than internal. Increased donations and church attendance become the barometer of success. Scriptural and doctrinal faithfulness are ignored or sacrificed in favor of the cult of personality. In the world we live in, appearances are everything, so a man who has laid aside the craft of pastoring and adopted an entrepreneurial approach to ministry really can't afford to pay much attention to the invisible side of things. There's just one problem with that approach: God's kingdom grows from the inside out. External growth depends and hinges around the invisible gifts of the Holy Spirit. As Jesus explained to Pilate, he was no threat to Caesar since his kingdom is not of this world (John 18:36). Though the gospel of Christ has great power to save, his kingdom grows quietly, almost imperceptibly, more like yeast than dynamite (Luke 13:20–21). If you bake bread with dynamite you have a very messy kitchen. Yet the temptation of Christ's church in every generation is to look to things more externally dynamic and impressive than internally transforming and pervasive.

To the extent that a hyperactive pastor still does what he's been given to do, albeit in a perfunctory way, souls are won and tended. God's Spirit works through means, not men, after all. It's not a pastor's inner disposition or attitude that lends efficacy to Christ's gospel, which always remains the power of God for salvation to everyone who believes (Rom 1:16). Yet the net effect of continually driving himself to a higher and higher level of output is crushing spiritually speaking. The hyperactive pastor has the same perpetual dread of failure as the man who has given up on ministry. Inwardly he's convinced he's driving himself toward greater achievement, but in reality he's driving himself into the ground. Worse, he's setting himself up for spectacular disaster. We've seen all too many clergy in America who have built elaborate spiritual fiefdoms for themselves and attracted thousands of followers, only to see their ministries unravel or crash and burn in very public moral or ethical failures.

But it doesn't have to be that way. There's always hope for those who have fallen prey to the pastoral depletion syndrome, no matter which stage they're in. Just as there is healing and recovery for pastors who have resigned their call, there is help for pastors who have become hyperactive robots in ministry too. It's called repentance, a good New Testament word that means change. Divinely ordered change, which is the right kind of change. Change rooted and grounded in God's mighty work of judgment and grace. Repentance embraces both contrition (sorrow over sin) and faith (firm trust in God). Turning our backs on both sin and hurt, we cling to Christ instead and in him find a new mind and new heart that brings a whole new life. That's the promise for every Christian, and the call perpetually goes out to one and all: "The time is fulfilled, and the kingdom of God is at hand; repent and believe in the gospel." (Mark 1:15).

Thank God, Jesus makes good on that promise of his to pastors as well. For every wounded soul who has given up on ministry and left his calling there is not only cleansing and healing, but a whole new life ahead. And for those deluded men who are foolishly trying to treat their pastoral depletion by throwing themselves with redoubled effort into increasing hyperactivity, there's hope as well. Repentance is not just a one-time thing. God is forever calling us back to the basics of word and Spirit rather than the misbelief and idolatry of popularity and success. We're all recovering sin addicts. Daily calling out our misbeliefs and naming our idols, we regularly turn from our sins and flee our prevailing temptations to find new life in Christ Jesus our Lord.

Though habits of sin die hard, it's possible to reawaken and culti-vate a renewed pastoral *habitus*. It will take time and effort, of course, and lots of help from colleagues and mentors in ministry, but then whoever said ministry would be easy? Certainly not Jesus: "If anyone would come after me, let him deny himself and take up his cross daily and follow me. For whoever would save his life will lose it, but who-ever loses his life for my sake will save it" (Luke 9:23–24). Not pleas-ant any way you look at it, but still quite the bargain, don't you agree?

INTERVENTION AND TREATMENT

There you have it: the three stages of depletion. I wish I could say they are rare, but experience teaches me that at any given time in ministry every one of us lies somewhere along this continuum of dysfunction. You saw what Lucas Woodford's misbeliefs did to him in chapter one. Don't become another casualty of the depletion syndrome. Use this chapter as a mirror, won't you? Take a long, hard, honest look at your life and inner disposition in light of what I've laid out here for you. Then take action. Don't try this alone. If you're in the early stages of depletion, seek intervention. If you've come to the latter stages, seek treatment. In both cases you'll need help. Thank God there are people who can help. But you will need to seek them out.

Humans are complex creations, with bodies, minds, and spir-its. Seek medical care to tackle physical conditions that impact you mentally and spiritually. An assessment by a mental health professional will help you address symptoms of anxiety or depression—very common ailments among us pastors, by the way. And here's a little known fact: Every pastor needs a pastor. If you're anywhere along the spectrum of this depletion dysfunction—whether confusion, desperation, or capitulation—there's help for you in Christ Jesus. He places his sure and certain word in the mouth of brother pastors to speak into your ears and sink deeply into your heart and soul so you can live again. Trust me; I've seen it happen before my very eyes.

It's been my privilege over the years to speak Christ's healing word to many bruised and broken pastors, men who lived for months or years in quiet, lonely desperation. Most of them were functional, though some were on the brink of disaster. But all of them lived daily right on the edge of despair. Symptoms varied widely from a nagging sense of inadequacy through chronic fear to abject failure. I heard stories that broke my heart: men who tried so desperately to please everyone that they had nothing left to give, men so incapacitated that they preached borrowed sermons week after week, men who were walking zombies, or who lived Hulk-like atop a volcano of simmering rage they could barely contain.

Many of these men were greatly helped by counseling from a licensed therapist. But no counselor could give the aid and comfort I was able to provide: as a called and ordained servant of Christ and by his authority to forgive them all their sins, to deliver balm and comfort for their wounds in Christ's shed blood, to intercede for them before God's throne of grace, to bless them with peace and consolation in the name of the holy Trinity. Before my own eyes I saw transformation begin as these men moved incrementally from grief to comfort, from fear to confidence, and then from despair to hope.

Not that I had anything in myself to give, mind you. Like you in your own pastoral calling, I simply was Christ's ear to hear their pain and then his mouth to speak his word, to pray his healing, to bestow his blessing. And there is healing and blessing in Christ for you, believe you me.

So don't be a lone ranger in ministry. Be brave enough to ask for help when you know you need it. Christ Jesus knows your pain and struggle, and he loves you enough to a give you a brother or father in ministry to come alongside, to listen to your aching heart and then speak his word of life and hope into your ears. I can tell you this: When you seek out pastoral help you will immensely benefit not just your calling and your congregation; if you're married, your wife and family will notice the difference too.

But the life you save may be your own.

Notes

1. Paul D. Borden, *Direct Hit: Aiming Real Leaders at the Mission Field* (Nashville: Abingdon Press, 2006), 34.

2. Thom S. Rainer, *Breakout Churches: Discover How to Make the Leap* (Grand Rapids: Zondervan, 2005), 64.

3. Jock E. Ficken, *Change: Learning to Lead and Living to Tell About It* (Lima, OH: Fairway Press), 21.

4. Lance Ford, *Unleader: Reimagining Leadership ... and Why We Must* (Kansas City: Beacon Hill Press, 2012), 21.

5. Ford, *Unleader*, 180.

6. Significant population decline occasionally calls for churches to make hard decisions, redirecting resources, consolidating ministries, or even closing congregations when necessary for the sake of expanding the Lord's mission in a given area.

7. *The New Testament in Modern English*, trans. J. B. Phillips (New York: MacMillan, 1958).

8. Eugene H. Peterson, *Working the Angles: The Shape of Pastoral Integrity* (Grand Rapids: Eerdmans, 1987), 2.

Works Cited

Borden, Paul D. *Direct Hit: Aiming Real Leaders at the Mission Field*.
    Nashville: Abingdon Press, 2006.

Bradberry, Travis, and Jean Greaves. *Emotional Intelligence 2.0*. San Diego:
    TalentSmart, 2009.

Cloud, Henry. *Boundaries for Leaders: Results, Relationships, and Being
    Ridiculously in Charge*. San Francisco: Harper Business, 2013.

Collins, Jim. *Good to Great: Why Some Companies Make the Leap ... and
    Others Don't*. San Francisco: HarperCollins, 2001.

Covey, Stephen. *The 7 Habits of Highly Effective People: Powerful Lessons in
    Personal Change*. Simon and Schuster, 1989.

———. *First Things First*. New York: Simon and Schuster, 1994.

Crowe, Brandon D. *Every Day Matters: A Biblical Approach to Productivity*.
    Bellingham, WA: Lexham Press, 2020.

Dreher, Rod. *The Benedict Option: A Strategy for Christians in a Post-
    Christian Nation*. New York: Sentinel, 2017.

Ficken, Jock E. *Change: Learning to Lead and Living to Tell About It*. Lima,
    OH: Fairway Press.

Ford, Lance. *Unleader: Reimagining Leadership ... and Why We Must*.
    Kansas City: Beacon Hill Press, 2012.

George, Bill. *True North: Becoming an Authentic Leader*. San Francisco:
    Jossey-Bass, 2015.

Goleman, Daniel. *Emotional Intelligence: Why It Can Matter More Than IQ*.
    New York: Bantam, 1995.

Lencioni, Patrick. *The Five Dysfunctions of a Team: A Leadership Fable*. San
    Francisco: Jossey-Bass, 2002.

———. *Death By Meeting: A Leadership Fable ... about Solving the Most
    Painful Problem in Business*. San Francisco: Jossey-Bass, 2004.

———. *Politics, Silos, and Turf Wars: A Leadership Fable about Destroying
    the Barriers That Turn Colleagues into Competitors*. San Francisco:
    Jossey-Bass, 2006.

Luther, Martin. *The Large Catechism.*

Maxwell, John C. *The 21 Irrefutable Laws of Leadership: Follow Them and People Will Follow You.* Nashville: Thomas Nelson, 1998, 2007.

———. *The 17 Indisputable Laws of Teamwork: Embrace Them and Empower Your Team.* Nashville: Thomas Nelson, 2001.

———. *Everyone Communicates, Few Connect: What the Most Effective People Do Differently.* Thomas Nelson, 2010.

———. *The 5 Levels of Leadership: Proven Steps to Maximize Your Potential.* New York: CenterStreet, 2011.

Peterson, Eugene H. *Working the Angles: The Shape of Pastoral Integrity.* Grand Rapids: Eerdmans, 1987.

Pink, Daniel. *Drive: The Surprising Truth about What Motivates Us.* New York: Riverhead Books, 2009.

Rainer, Thom S. *Breakout Churches: Discover How to Make the Leap.* Grand Rapids: Zondervan, 2005.

Rath, Tom. *Strengths Finder 2.0.* New York: Gallup Press, 2007.

Sinek, Simon. *Start with Why: How Great Leaders Inspire Everyone to Take Action.* New York: Penguin, 2009.

———. *Leaders Eat Last: Why Some Teams Pull Together and Others Don't.* New York: Penguin, 2017.

Stanley, Andy. *Making Vision Stick.* Grand Rapids: Zondervan, 2007.

The New Testament in Modern English. Translated by J. B. Phillips. New York: MacMillan, 1958.

Wiseman, Liz, with Greg McKeon. *Multipliers: How the Best Leaders Make Everyone Smarter.* San Francisco: Harper Business, 2010.

Woodford, Lucas V. *Commission, Great Confusion, or Great Confession? The Mission of the Holy Christian Church.* Eugene, OR: Wipf & Stock, 2012.

PASTORS CARE FOR A SOUL IN THE WAY A DOCTOR CARES FOR A BODY.

In a time when many churches have lost sight of the real purpose of the church, *The Care of Souls* invites a new generation of pastors to form the godly habits and practical wisdom needed to minister to the hearts and souls of those committed to their care.

"Pastoral theology at its best. Every pastor, and everyone who wants to be a pastor, should read this book."
—Timothy George, Founding Dean, Beeson Divinity School, Samford University; General Editor, Reformation Commentary on Scripture